The Penny Share Millionaire

The Penny Share Millionaire

The Ultimate Guide to Trading

Jacques Magliolo

BEP BUSINESS EXPERT PRESS

First published in 2017 by
Business Expert Press, LLC
222 East 46th Street, New York, NY 10017
www.businessexpertpress.com

ISBN-13: 978-1-63157-782-6 (paperback)
ISBN-13: 978-1-63157-748-2 (e-book)

Business Expert Press Finance and Financial Management Collection

Collection ISSN: 2331-0049 (print)
Collection ISSN: 2331-0057 (electronic)

Cover and interior design by S4Carlisle Publishing Services
Private Ltd., Chennai, India

First edition: 2017

10 9 8 7 6 5 4 3 2 1

Printed in the United States of America.

Dedication

To my wife Kathy Florence-Magliolo

Abstract

Trading shares takes courage and an understanding of trading psyche. This booklet outlines a set of rules to trade in a hostile and aggressive market, including:

- A comprehensive set of rules, outlined for pre-actual and post-trading.
- Fundamental analysis to create a filter to determine what to buy and what the fair value of a share is.
- Technical indicators to assess and determine timing strategies, such as entry and exit levels.
- Market timing strategies.

Keywords

buy, exit, fundamental analysis, JSE, microcap, Penny Shares, SEC, strategy, technical

Contents

Foreword

Penny stock trading is definitely not for everyone.

Those who are okay with riskier investments should give penny stock trading a try, but ensure that you have a sound strategy in place to limit that risk.

It is always recommended that you start slowly and build knowledge before building up your investments.

This book is effectively a Guide to trading small cap shares and is the culmination of queries made by clients about trading such shares, ideas about strategy in such markets and, simply, the dire and recognized need to expand options for novice traders. In a market dominated by blue chips around the world, picking a future winner today is exciting and, not to say the least, potentially profitable.

Recently, a client noted that he had not made as much money as when I recommended penny shares to clients between 2010 and 2014.

During those years, I was an editor of a magazine that concentrated on penny stocks.

And so I started to think about writing my 14th financial book. When I researched the subject of trading shares or derivatives, I realized that a Guide would be more effective to assist novice traders to pick winners in the small-cap market. In addition, the plan was to write a Guide to mentor novice traders and, at the same time, establish an easy-to-understand set of basic trading rules, both for short- and long-term traders.

Let me start by stating that performance of companies' shares on any stock market is part of everyday news, but it is often not easy to assess what really influences share prices, and why such news is often critical to market volatility. The basic economic principles of supply, demand, liquidity, transparency, and corporate governance obviously affect share prices and at times these are obvious, but what factors have the greatest influence and by how much is not always obvious or easily identifiable.

The information revealed in financial accounts is important, but are these the only variables worth considering? What about political factors, like war, terrorism, famine, and violent labor strikes? What about economic and business factors, such as interest rates and inflation, employment statistics, and monitory policy? Does technology influence share prices?

Every day, companies are releasing results. Every day, these offer opportunities for day traders and in particular to penny share traders. Yet, clients often tell me that when results have been released, the shares have already moved and any possible opportunities have disappeared.

They are quite correct. The market waits for no one and, unless you are ready with your Entry and Exit strategies in place before the market opens, those opportunities will have evaporated.

It is easy to see which companies are doing well once the company has released financial results, by which time shares have moved out from being undervalued and the trading Gap has been missed. Similarly, by the time a company's released financial performance is obviously poor, the share price has already fallen. If you could have a strategy and trading system that works at least 80% of the time, wouldn't you love to be a business owner without ever having to show up at work? Imagine if you could sit back, watch your securities trading company grow and collect the dividend payments as the money rolls in!

This situation might sound like a pipe dream, but it is closer to reality than you might think. I have personally trained and mentored people who had absolutely no idea how markets work. In one instance, a young policeman came to me because he "had to get out of the police force." Equipped with barely a high school diploma, today he teaches technical analysis for a living. A second example, an elderly woman came to me because she "couldn't live on her pension." Today, she too, is trading for a living, establishing her financial goals per month over the past 12 years.

When I started out as an analyst, a colleague said to me that there isn't another job anywhere in the world that enables you to build as much wealth over time as is possible in stockbroking as a trader.

The stock market is, without a doubt, one of the greatest tools ever invented for building wealth. Stocks are a part, if not the cornerstone, of any investment portfolio. When you start on your road to financial freedom, you need to have a solid understanding of stocks and how they trade on the stock market. Given the phenomenal tool that the internet has become, the trader that you want to be must ultimately be a global one, trading across borders, securities, and investment opportunities.

Remember that this book looks only at trading penny shares, but you must not forget that ultimately you should be building wealth with long-term investments and methods to take advantage of market anomalies with derivatives.

Trading penny shares is merely one tool that successful traders use.

There is, however, a lesson that needs to be expounded before you start down that road. Despite the complexities involved in analysis of bonds, futures, warrants, and shares, remember the following simple statement:

You need to develop just two skills to succeed as a trader:

- Trading without strategy based on solid information is committing financial suicide.
- Trading without understanding investor sentiment and risk involved in decision making is the road to failure.

So, the more complex the investment decision, the more information is required and the greater the understanding of the risk involved in making that decision.

Let me give you an example.

A well-known South African JSE Securities Exchange–listed company planned to expand into Zambia.

- Initially, analysis of this company involved analysis of global factors that affect this South African company, assessing local environmental factors (economic, business, political, and technological), trends and supply and demand for the share.
- The company was followed avidly by analysts and traders alike. Initially, the company share rose on improved investor sentiment.
- Remember that the company had not yet shown an increase in turnover by its planned expansion. The operative word was *PLANNED!*

- This provided traders with a Gap—the difference between share price and fair value. Those astute traders, who had researched and assessed (predicted) the planned expansion were able to ride the upswing in price.
- Now, the company finally moves into an area where there was very little official statistics and a highly volatile political setup. Remember that all the factors that had to be assessed still apply. The risk profile of investing in this company sky rocketed and the investment wealth potential became uncertain.
- Still no increase in profits, but expenses rose as the expansion became a reality. However, part of that reality was that the level of difficulties had not been properly quantified.
- Investors waited for an update and, when the company became quiet on the issue, traders sold the share. This provided traders with another opportunity.

Over the last few decades, the average person's interest in the stock market has grown exponentially. What was once the domain of the rich has now turned into a vehicle of choice for everyone to grow their personal wealth. This demand coupled with advances in trading technology has opened up the markets so that today nearly anybody can own stock market securities, whether shares, Futures or Forex. And they can do this themselves; without the assistance of a stockbroker.

Despite their popularity, however, most people don't fully understand how to trade, or how to trade by using an online brokerage house. Unfortunately, too many potential traders rely on conversations with friends and so-called experts; those who proclaim to understand why shares move, but have no formal training or experience in the market.

These are people who often have get-rich-quick mentalities, which has been especially prevalent during this seven year bull-run. Many novice traders think that the stock market is the magic answer to instant wealth with no risk. Stocks can (and do) create massive amounts of wealth, but they are not without risk. The only solution to this is education; have knowledge and understand the factors that influence the market within which the company operates and also internal company matters.

The key to protecting yourself in the stock market is to understand where you are putting your money.

My aim is to write a series of books that Guide traders and these will cover many elements of the trading spectrum, including forex, bonds, and Futures; from basics to more comprehensive trading strategies, which would include fundamental and technical analysis.

This Guide is thus the first in a series.

Jacques Magliolo
jacques@bci.za.com
www.bci.za.com
2017

"Markets are constantly in a state of uncertainty and flux and money is made by discounting the obvious and betting on the unexpected,"

—George Soros

Introduction

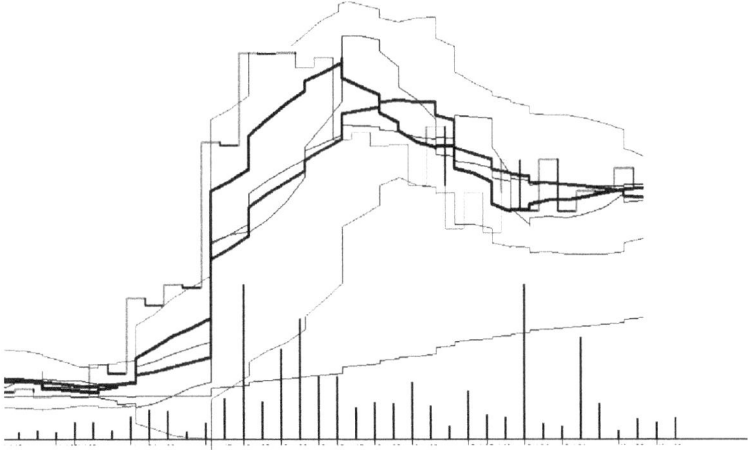

Looks impressive, doesn't it?

Now imagine if you had to take the above graph and add due diligence, business structures, regulatory issues, and accounting forensics? On top of that, imagine trading in a global environment with a multitude of cultures, languages, ethics (or lack thereof), corporate governance, time differences, currency risk profiles, and conglomerates, which rule the global corporate environment with a staggering hostility and ruthlessness that is backed by billions of dollars.

To the point, in fact, that traders around the world have had to rethink their entire way of running their portfolios. Do they have the requisite level of understanding of the economics, business, socio-political nuances, and technological know-how to undertake trading ventures in the future? Are the old, tried and tested methods, fundamentals and technical theories enough to survive and prosper under such conditions?

Do traders need to rethink what they buy and sell?

Do they need to take a step back and assess how they will continue to operate and achieve requisite levels of profit? My experience suggests that there isn't really need to panic. The problem, however, is that traders need to do things right the first time. There simply is no short cut to prospering in a global marketplace.

Too many traders spend too much time trying to resolve *every* problem that occurs within a market and are thus not prepared for the rapidly changing condition within which they trade. As a corporate consultant, I'm repeatedly approached to resolve such issues for local traders. So, at the first meeting, my first questions are always the same: "Do you have a long-term wealth strategy? Do you have a medium-term portfolio to take advantage of market anomalies? What is your cash flow strategy?

These seem like simple and obvious questions, but you would be surprised by the answers. These range from "*do I need to have strategies*" to "*I trade with gut feel.*"

These issues may seem obvious and not pertinent to you. Or are they?

Some years ago, I was commissioned to restructure a client's portfolio, worth over US$20 million. My immediate impression was one of shock. The portfolio was unbalanced, not diversified and, simply, featured too many stocks that were not tradable, illiquid, and some close to termination.

When I pointed these out to him, he said: "I followed my advisor's recommendations. He is a nice guy and I trust him."

Trust is important in dealing with your stockbroker/portfolio manager, but whether he or she are "nice" or not is just too ridiculous to contemplate. His portfolio was a disaster and a major clean-up was undertaken.

The obvious is not always easy to see. This is the main reason why I have launched my own securities' mentoring program. The methodology outlined in the program enables traders to initiate, plan and take control of their portfolios and to deliver strategies that work.

A program should include the following elements:

	Phases	Content	Aim
1	Portfolio management	Developing a strategy to reduce risk through diversification and portfolio balancing	DETERMINE WHAT SECURITIES TO BUY
2	Fundamental share price valuation	Ability to calculate a share price's current fair value and to forecast a share price trading range into the future using investor sentiment and a company's financials.	
3	Develop a Share Filter System	Develop a personal strategy that enables the trainee to acquire securities quickly and efficiently	
4	Technical analysis	Develop personal use of triggers to enter/exit trades	DETERMINE WHEN TO BUY SECURITIES
5	Virtual Trading	The practical side of the program to identify any weaknesses prior to trading	WHAT & WHEN TO BUY
6	Actual Trading	Assist trainee to conduct actual trading	

Today, I mentor 12 clients at any one time, taking them through various levels to enable them to develop portfolio strategies, create a securities' filter system to select shares to trade and establish a technical analysis system to acquire securities.

This Guide will outline how to trade penny shares, both as a day trader and for the long term. And the aim is to enable you to trade successfully, taking into account that such success must be achieved in today's hostile and extremely ruthless competitive world, where the four environmental factors of economics, business, politics, and technology influence markets at a rapidly growing rate.

This Guide will expose your historic trading structural weaknesses and potential losses.

By applying basic processes, tools, and techniques shown in this book, you can maximize performance and ensure optimum (and safer) trading results.

The main reason for writing this Guide has been a perceived widening gap between current trading theory and practice and the dire need for global strategy, knowledge, and coordinated planning when undertaking any trade, whatever the size or cost.

CHAPTER 1

General Terms, Warnings, and Other Info

"One of the funny things about the stock market is that every time one person buys, another sells, and both think they are astute."
—William Feather (1889–1981),
an American Publisher and Author

Definitions

What Are Penny Shares?

Shares that are low-priced and have a small market capitalization are known as penny stocks. This doesn't mean that these shares cost only one cent each? The US Securities Exchange Commission (The SEC) has a set of rules pertaining to penny shares (See Appendices), but it is sufficient to state that a penny share can be defined as:

Any stock trading at or under US$5.

Actually, depending whether you are assessing the London Exchange or the Johannesburg Securities Exchange (JSE), the terms are interchangeable and must be noted that some confusion is made when an Exchange is denoted as a "Small Cap Exchange" such as the JSE's Alternative Exchange (AltX) or the London Stock Exchange's Alternative Investment Market (AIM). Most shares on the AltX and AIM trade above what traders consider as penny shares.

Therefore, it is more accurate and technically correct to state that a small-cap or microcap stock is based on their market capitalizations, while penny shares are deemed to be viewed on price.

While definitions vary across different world exchanges, the SEC states that stock with a market capitalization between US$50 and US$300 million is a microcap.

At the outset, let me state that trading penny shares is risky. Many novice traders have the mistaken opinion that it is easier to make profits on a penny share than on a blue chip.

The logic is as follows:

> It is easier to see a share price double from two cents to four cents than it is for a US$100 to double to US$200.

Except that a share that is trading at two cents may never rise to those levels. Take for instance, a company with the follow statistics:

- Share price: two cents
- Shares in issue: 500 million
- Attributable profit: US$100 million
- Price earnings: 10 times

For the company's share to double, the company would have to see the following happen:

- The company would have to double its profit to US$200 million; or
- The company's price earnings (PE) ratio would have to double to 20 times.

Calculations:

A) **Fair Value**
- SHARE PRICE $= PE \times EPS$
- THEREFORE: SHARE PRICE $= 10 \times$ (US$100 million divided by 500 million)
- THEREFORE: SHARE PRICE $= 10 \times 0.2$ cents
- THEREFORE: SHARE PRICE $= 2$ cents

For the share price to double:

- PE RISES to 20 times:
  - PE = SHARE PRICE DIVIDED BY EPS
  - PE = 4 DIVIDED BY 0.2
  - PE = 20 TIMES

Both are extremely unlikely.

Benefits of Penny Share Trading

If you have a portfolio of US$20 000, and wish to invest 10% in DAY trading opportunities, you would be limited by the effect of brokerage, tax, and other securities costs.

As such, US$5000 per trade would be the least amount to be effective in trading. This amount is not a sufficient spread of risk in speculative situations, but investing in penny shares, you create a better spread of risk and achieve a diversified portfolio.

Note that if you trade regularly, even if your portfolio is a small amount of funds, you could be classified as a share trader and pay full tax rate of 45% or more, depending on the countries' tax rate.

Disadvantages

Over time, we have witnessed listed companies, with poorly traded shares, suddenly rocket as corporate announcements are made of, among other, restructuring and new contracts being granted. There is always the potential that traders will see their investments rise to unbelievable levels.

There is the possibility of finding undervalued situations and to position the portfolio for an upswing in a sector or overall market. Traders under such conditions must inhibit patience, but also have the funds to wait for the investment to perform as expected. Funds tied into a potential gain without analysis is an opportunity cost.

Remember the Axiom: A Successful Trader is one who has knowledge and Discipline.

Trading on Media and Other Market Noise

The key to any successful trading strategy is to understand how leading and lagging indicators work. For instance, if the Exchange is the Leading Indicator of the economy, then any environmental factor that doesn't alter this fundamental principle is the Market Noise.

Environmental Factors:

- Politics, including the influence of labor and labor unions
- Economics, including cross border trade
- Business, including mergers and acquisitions
- Technology

If one of the above factors moves a market or share, then it is Market Noise and the share may be deemed to be a trading opportunity. It must be noted that penny shares and other microcap stocks tend to display poor information that is difficult to obtain.

Note:

- **The New York Stock Exchange and Nasdaq:**
  - Companies listed on the pink sheets are not required to file financials with the SEC.
  - These are therefore often not scrutinized by analysts, professional traders or portfolio managers.
  - In addition, these securities often do not have to fulfil minimum standard requirements to remain on the exchange.
  - Many of these companies were previously listed on a major exchange, but moved to one of these smaller exchanges because they couldn't maintain minimum standards as prescribed by the SEC.
- The JSE's Venture Capital Market and the Development Capital Market.
  - Denoted as "Graveyard sectors"
  - Not traded often.

- ○ Many companies in these sectors are considered penny shares.
- ○ Opportunities exist if these companies move to the JSE's Main Board or the AltX.

New, Old, or Dead

Many microcaps are either new companies with little or no history and represent a trading opportunity or they are near bankruptcy and may represent a breakup value.

In either case the risk that a value is found is often difficult as information is usually scarce.

True Liquidity

Liquidity is when you can sell a penny share after you have bought it.

- So, if you buy the share, will you be able to exit the trade?
- A stock should have continued trades and at least 400,000 trades a week.
- Low liquidity does provide traders with opportunities when:
  - ○ Market makers move the share as part of their marketing.
  - ○ When rumors move the share on potential corporate deals.
  - ○ When the share is hyped illegally.

So, how can you tell if a share is liquid?

One simple method is to use ratio analysis, but more specifically, ratios that assess the company's Operating Cash Flow. Penny share traders find this ratio of particular importance as it assesses the amount of cash-derived from operations as a percentage of current liabilities.

Effectively, the ratio illustrates how many times the generated cash flow will cover the company's short-term debt.

$$\text{Operating Cash Flow Ratio} = \frac{\text{Cash Flow from Operations}}{\text{Current Liabilities}}$$

Here is the logic for investing in companies with strong operating cash flows:

- The thumb-rule is that income/turnover has to rise at a greater rate than expenses for the ratio to increase. Using this logic, higher income should result in higher profits, which—when divided by the company's shares in issue, will result in a higher earnings per share (EPS).

- ○ As such, if you use an unchanged PE ratio, the share price should increase.

- Microcompanies that increase income do not have to issue more shares to fund growth or expansion.
  - ○ Remember that any increase in a company's issued share capital will result in a lower share price.
- Higher cash flows than expenses result in increased profitability, which often equates to expansion, which in turn should result in higher future profits and thus share price.

Trader Warnings

Why Some Traders Fail

- Inadequately defined trading strategies.
- Enter trades without analysis.
- Avoid thorough fundamental analysis.
- Improper technical analysis to determine entry levels.
- Failing to keep to Exit strategies.
- Focus only on penny stocks with high volume.
- No Stop Loss Strategy.

Questions: Ask Yourself Before You Start

- What profits do you need to make?
- What is your Break-even?
- What is your strategy to achieve this cash flow?

Simple Trader's Checklist

- What is your plan?
- Do you have a trading plan?
- Have you conducted Industry strengths, weaknesses, opportunities, and threats (SWOT)?

- Have you conducted portfolio and diversification analysis?
- What fundaments and technical analysis have you completed?
- Set out the structure of your portfolio.
- Are you going to establish a long-term portfolio?
- Are you going to establish a medium-term higher risk Futures portfolio?
- Are you going to use hedging strategies?
- Have you written your trades down in a Trading Journal?

Strick Rules to Obey

	Rules	Take Note
1	Greed and Fear	I have heard traders say that a particular penny share would rise by 1000%, turning you into an *Instant Millionaire*. Too many sad people. Too many disillusioned traders. You listen to such hype and you will not be a trader for long. The lesson: Don't let Greed and Fear rule your trading life.
2	Have an Exit Strategy	Trading penny shares can generate 15% returns almost daily, but profits turn to losses if you don't have an Exit Strategy.
3	Keep to Your Plan	The secret to success is always: Have a plan, make a decision, and then follow through. If you create a trading plan, but then don't follow through—you are just gambling in the hope of making profits. These rules should be flexible, but used as guidelines.

CHAPTER 2

30 Years of Observations

"The stock market is like a small row boat on a rough sea, bouncing around as it drifts, whereas the macro economy is like a large ocean liner, very ponderous and difficult to manoeuvre, but without such a rough journey."

—Sir Clive Granger (1934–2009), British Economist

At some point, you will make a mistake and your trade will end up as a loss. At some point, you will do everything right and still make a loss. I started my stockbroking career in 1990, and as you can imagine, I have seeing significant changes, from the start on online trading to the introduction of a vast variety of securities. If there is one lesson that I have learnt in all this time is that knowledge is true power if you are to prosper as a trader and, even more importantly, discipline is critical.

All knowledge is useless without the capability to carry out your own defined strategy. Note that when I speak of knowledge I am not just referring to trading rules, but in understanding and observing human behavior. Look around you, and observe what people are doing, what they are buying and when they are buying goods and services. Look for new trends. Look for what is changing the status quo. Open your eyes and build knowledge and with that will come experience and street wise capabilities not taught in text books.

These are unbreakable truths, but how you handle your mistakes or losses or profits for that matter, is what will ultimately result in continuous profitable trades or—more pertinently—enable you to become a full time trader.

While professional traders expect to make mistakes and losses at times, it is the prepared and wise trader who insures against such mistakes, and although failure teaches a valuable lesson, it is how you react to market conditions, that provides the best model for success.

You are not unique in the world of global stock markets. All traders experience difficulties common to all those involved in the market. Consequently, success is not the preserve of the great and you, as a trader, must always be the architect of your own fortune, take responsibility for all your trades and actions. The advantage novice traders have today is that they can acquire the services of a mentor, who can be the architect for your entrée into the market.

The Penny Share Millionaire is intended to be a guide and a work of reference to which novice traders can turn to for help in setting up their trading plans and to organize and develop their trading business. It should also be used to sort problems that continually confront them and which has been set out in their trading journal. Every effort has been made to avoid technicalities and jargon, and to explain in plain, unmistakable language, not only the best thing to do, but the best way to do it.

It is hoped that the work will be useful to both novice and the more advanced trader—for the latter should remember that he or she cannot stand still; the market has an amazing ability to continually change its rules and its services and products.

Unless a novice trader is continually on the watch for improvements, in these days of hostile and aggressive competition, he/she is certainly not to go forward. This is a practical way of stating the important economic law that *Profits tend to disappear.*

The advice from experts is for novice traders, at the beginning of their trading journey, to admit that there are some people who are not suited by temperament and character to enter trading. Find a mentor and establish what kind of trader you are more suited to. You may be more of an investor than trader?

It is wise for novice traders to know their limitations and to be prepared to accept discouragements, from family and friends.

Vast Opportunities of Trade Around the World

The Trillion Dollar Club – Your Ultimate Playing Field

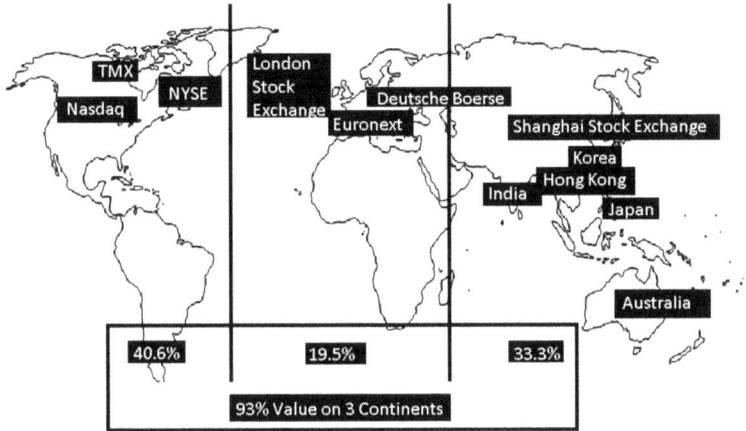

As an example of how markets change, in 1990 the JSE's trading value per day was less than US$2 million. Today it averages over US$70 million. According to the World Federation of Exchanges, more than 50% of all income generated by stock exchanges around the world is derived from small-cap markets.

The whole essence of the trading business is personality. To be a successful trader today, you need to take cognisance of the many changes that will occur in markets around the world and the influence that these may have on your portfolio.

The trader can organize and create complex computer systems and models to assess and determine sources of supply and demand, price trends, and market trends, but you cannot create a system that will automatically run itself.

Remember that shares are determined by a company's financials and investor sentiment. It is the latter that takes understanding of the human psyche to make you a really successful trader.

A next important fact that makes this age favorable to being a trader is that our lives become increasingly complex, particularly with globalization of markets. With each addition to the markets of securities and cross border opportunities arise countless new trades.

Always Room for the Penny Share Trader

In spite of the growth of multiple types of securities, there are millions more people entering the trading arena than ever before. This means that investor sentiment has started being a more important element in the movement of share prices than ever before.

Remember this truism: The increase in different types of securities around the world has only one goal: *To quickly return shares to fair value.*

Therefore, if a share has fallen by 3% overnight, should you buy the share?

Take heed of the following questions:

Questions	
1	Should I trade today?
2	If yes—then what shares meet my personal fundamental strategy?
3	If yes—are these shares over or undervalued
4	If technical analysis suggests an opportunity—What are my entry and exit strategies

Be Different—Don't Follow the Crowd

Remember:

- Everyone has the same systems and access to information that you do.
- To beat the market, you have to be different.
- Be different in your thinking does not only mean being contrarian.
- Create your own statistical databases and indices.
- For instance, there are nine listed pharmaceutical companies on the JSE. Yet only four are listed under a Pharmaceutical sector.
- Creating your own Medical Sector Index would give you statistics that would be different to other traders'.
- Learn to interpret information quickly and how such information will affect shares.
- Following what other traders do, will get you average returns— often declining profits.

Implications of Overtrading

The temptation is easy to overtrade and the worst of it is that it never looks like overtrading until you are right in it—trying to handle 15 trades. At most, look at having only four open positions at any one time. This is what Scalpers do, to great effect.

When markets are rising and profits are regular, then the business of stockbroking looks easy and your decision to become a trader is confirmed. You can brag to your former colleagues, your family and friends. However, when the market turns against you and losses surpass your profits, you may be forced to draw on your capital. When this happens, your ability to make money on a consistent basis is truly compromised.

The following is a basic outline of successful traders' strategies:

1. Have a long-term portfolio as your retirement fund-
   a. Build a portfolio of dividend income companies.
   b. Regularly review and maintain the portfolio.
2. Create a medium-term, high-risk portfolio
   a. Use derivatives to hedge your long-term portfolio.
   b. Use derivatives to trade market anomalies.
3. Create a day trading portfolio
   a. Use penny shares as your monthly cash flow.
   b. Any extra funds achieved above your required "salary" should be ploughed back into your long-term portfolio.

When the market is in a strong bull run, some novice traders forget their own pre-established trading rules, to quickly find themselves overtrading. Be aware and take immediate and corrective action. This may not always be easy.

In some instances, sitting tight may be your only strategy.

Neglected Value Situations

Most major countries' stock exchanges have a set of Blue Chip shares that the brokers and professional traders and portfolio managers concentrate on. These exchanges even have names for these, including the JSE Top 40, the CAC-40 (benchmark index for funds on the French Bourse) and the DAX 30, which represents the top 30 listed German companies.

In fact, not only do many brokers concentrate on these top companies, they often also limit their research to these companies. This in essence ignores penny shares and other microcaps. These shares are therefore often neglected and at times may represent outstanding value. This effectively means that such shares are undervalued relative to their true value.

Basic guidelines, therefore, to assess such companies should include valuation on these shares based on a thorough analysis of the financial statements, including:

- The company must have a strong balance sheet
- The company must have good prospects
- Must have experienced management
- Must have numerous contracts
- The company's share price should be well supported, be liquid and tradable, that is, it must have a sound price track record.

Assess those rare situations where the opportunity is very high and the risk is very low. The latter is assessed by analysing investor sentiment. The easiest way to determine this is to download the price earnings (PE) ratio of a company over the past three years.

Company PE to Sector Averages

To determine the true fair value of a share, you need to assess what the market sentiment is toward that stock. If a share is trading at 500 cents, but the market believes that this is too expensive—what do you think will happen to the price? So, establish a Buy and Sell range based on market expectation. I call this the Expense Ratio.

How do you do that?

The first step is to determine what the market sentiment is toward a sector.

SELL SEGMENT

Average PE

BUY SEGMENT

The above graph is the Retail Sector.

The first step is to find that Expense Ratio.

Some software packages allow you to download PE ratios of sectors and shares. Make sure that your package permits you to do so. Download the PE ratio into an excel spreadsheet.

- Step 1: find the average PE ratio
- Step 2: plot this relative to the general PE ratio

The above indicates that the sector is cheaper than the average. As such, market sentiment is returning to that sector and offers an opportunity.

The Single Company

At a glance and without any technical analysis—the following share shows that the share has reached the bottom of a support level and could bounce. However, without knowing market expectations, what do we do?

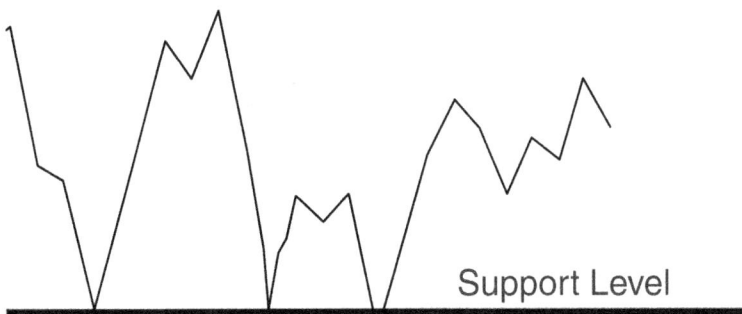

Support Level

- We look at the Expense Ratio.

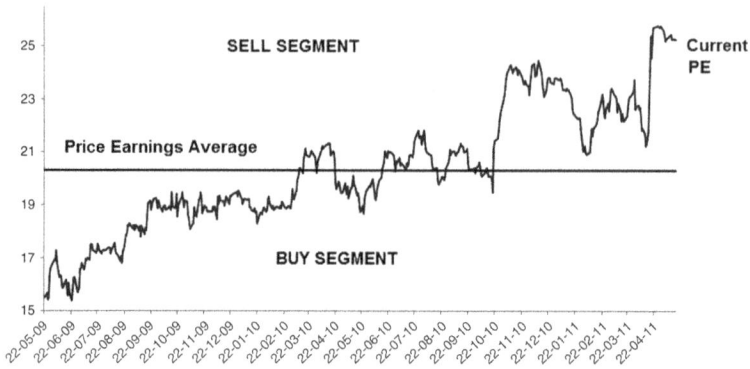

Now, the Expense Ratio highlights that the retailer's share is expensive and above the average PE. As such, the share is not a buy. The question is whether this company is cheaper or more expensive than its main competitor.

Company PE versus Competitor PE

The next phase is to look at Company A relative to a close competitor, Company B. Assume that Retailer B is also considered to be expensive and not a Buy. However, when you divide the PE ratio of Company B to that of Company A, you get the following:

Result:

- Retailer A is cheaper than Retailer B and below the average PE.
- This indicates that—if a trader wishes to be in a retail stock— Company A is still a better buy.

This takes us to assessment of the share price.

Share Price Analysis

Traders must run scans to find some potential trades. Specifically, they need to assess for stocks that:

- Need to be in strong bull or bear trends
- Meet the criteria as set out in this chapter.

Using this trading strategy, traders use the Williams %R to assess whether they should go long or short. Once that happens, then need to run through their watch lists to find potential trades. The ability to establish a solid watch list is important to expedite trades.

The first step is to understand the companies that you have placed in your watch list. For instance, if you have assessed that the chemical industry is the one to be in, then you need to find companies that fits that criteria. You will find many misconceptions in the market. With lack of solid data, you will invest in the wrong company.

A method that some traders adopt is to compare the company's share price with its 12 month high and low and its net asset value.

The following table is an example:

Name	Nature of Business	Share Price			NAV	Buy-Sell
		Price	12 Month High	12 Month Low		
Company 1						
Company 2						

(continued)

Name	Nature of Business	Share Price			NAV	Buy-Sell
		Price	12 Month High	12 Month Low		
Company 3						
Company 4						
Company 5						

The benefit of doing the above exercise is that—at a glance—you will be able to see and assess a company's share relative to itself. For instance, if Company 1's share price is 120 cents and this is close to its 12 month high of 130 cents, is the share still worth buying?

Well, if the share price is still below the 160 cents net asset value, it may be? It triggers possible shares in the watch list.

Once you have made the trade, stick to your analysis. Use your exit strategy to either take profits or losses, but don't be swayed by market news and innuendo.

The success of this trading strategy relies on ability to find good stocks to trade within reasonable ranges.

The penny share market is sometime inefficient in correcting price movements, which provides opportunities for investors with the mental make up to go against the popular prevailing wisdom by buying under-valued shares and then with the patience and financial strength to hold them until the market comes to its senses.

In penny shares, management is often key to the company's success and thus the share price.

CHAPTER 3

Are You Suited to Penny Share Trading

"Short term traders, who only concentrate on the "what" (what to buy) and not on the "when" (when to strike), will be trading on a very short term basis indeed."

—Oliver Velez & Greg Capra, 2000. Tools and Tactics for the Master Day Trader: Battle-Tested Techniques for Day, Swing, and Position Traders, McGraw Hill

It is easy to say that *"I will become a Millionaire Penny Share Trader."*

But not easy to implement.

Let me explain. You may have all the knowledge to trade, in-depth understanding of economic cycles, and strong fundamental and technical analytical skills, but you may not have the personality or character to succeed as a penny share trader, which takes courage and patience.

There is an old stockbroking Axiom: *"To succeed in the market you need Discipline and Knowledge."*

Over the years, I have added to that Axiom. Once you have used that knowledge and discipline to select your penny share, THEN WITHOUT IMMEDIATE FOLLOW THROUGH YOUR INTENDED RESULTS ARE DOUBTFUL.

All the knowledge in the world means nothing if you don't have the discipline to carry out your own strategy, time your entries, and resist greed and panic during your trading hours. So, I have devised a basic questionnaire for you to determine what type of trader you really are. Note that this is a measure and will change over time. It doesn't mean that it is set in stone. I have mentored young aggressive people who believed that they were suited to day trading, only to end up as long-term investors. The opposite has also been true.

Build Your Own Psychological Trading Profile

When it comes to the mental game of trading, it's important to look at your own strengths and weaknesses—and to be honest in your assessment. No one can tell you about you, better than you can, but I stress that day trading is not for everyone. The following psychological profile should get you thinking about personality, risk tolerance, and lifestyle. This may help you assess whether you really have the temperament to be a day trader or you're better suited to being a long-term investor. If you enjoy strategizing and have the patience to keep to that strategy and the discipline and not change stop losses, you may find that you're a day trader at heart.

Note: The following psychological profile is only a guide to help assess risk tolerance and attraction to trading. Your score is in no way a guarantee of success or failure, but it is a start.

Questions	Never	Rarely	Sometimes	Often	Always
Points	1	2	3	4	5
Markets shouldn't move irrationally. I don't like this about markets.					
I desire to only make large profits					
My daily strategy is to apply gut feel					
I want people to see me as a Millionaire Trader					
Discipline is an outdated philosophy					
Every trade has the same chance of success					

Long-term trends are easier to identify and forecast					
I am drawn to the day trading lifestyle					
The market is just a game					
I trade to prove that I can succeed					
I will make profits					
I am patient and believe in my strategy, even when I have to hold trading positions					
I love scalping to exploit short-term market swings					
A day trading career is easy					
I live on the edge and on adrenaline when I trade					
I enter trades because I know I'm right					
I don't believe in exit strategies or stop loss theories					
I believe and follow market noise and expert analysis					
I am analytical and plan every trading day before the market opens					
I am a risk taker					
I learn quickly and take advantage of similar trends in future					
I believe in taking immediate action when I lose a trade					
I hate stable markets					
TOTAL					

Add your score and review your profile as follows.

Score	Conclusions	Result
+80	Your ideas of trading are unrealistic and thus not consistent with the realities of stresses incurred when trading.	It is suggested that you reassess your trading goals.
60 to 80	You are risk averse	You are more suited to being a long-term trader or investor, than being a day trader.
40 to 60	You are aggressive and have solid trader instincts	You are well suited to becoming a penny share day trader.
20 to 40	Too indecisive	You are not suited to being a penny share trader.
−20	Your skills lie outside the field of trading	Try another field in the markets, such as portfolio management or analysis.

Historic Day Trading Psychology Lessons

As a means of building a physiological profile it is pertinent and particularly relevant for penny share traders to assess and take cognisance of the following psychological traits that day traders inhibit.

- **Influence is two ways.** Trading affects psychology and psychology affects trading. Poor trading skills will result in poor trades, which will result in heightened stress. In turn, stress increases the level of mistakes traders make in the market. Mentally prepare yourself before you enter the market and have a strategy to remove (as much as possible) risk and emotion from trading.
- **Everything is connected–Everyone is affected.** Whether you are successful or not, you will experience emotion disruption during a trading day. There is not a single method of trading that is infallible, that is, all trading methods will experience consecutive losses at some stage. These can occur during bear or bull markets. Avoid significant losses by having stop loss methods in place.

- **Personal emotions will affect you.** Traders tend to associate emotions only to market and market movements. Take account of personal issues such as ill health and family-related emotions and never forget that external issues can have mega influences on your mental state, like terror attacks on your country. Traders are just as susceptible to overconfidence during profitable runs as underconfidence when experiencing consecutive losses.
- **Be prudent.** While confidence is a positive trait for day traders, one of the quickest ways to financial ruin is to continuously place your whole portfolio at risk with every trade. If trades are too large (as a percentage of the whole portfolio), they can create exaggerated swings between profit and losses, which in turn results in emotional swings.
- **Get knowledge**: Without training and practice, the day trader lacks the skills to survive in a hostile and aggressive business like being a trader.
- **In markets, change is the only constant**: Trading patterns, ratios, share prices, volatility of investor sentiment, and market trends continually change, moving between overvalued to underpriced. The successful trader has plans in place to take advantage of any market conditions.
- **Everyone learns**: Markets are continually changing, offering new products and systems. The best traders go through a process of continually relearning and absorbing the elements of change.
- **Differences, Gaps and opportunities.** Markets, sectors, companies, and securities continually change and the differences between them at times become wider, at other times minimised gaps. Some markets are more volatile than others; some have more distinct patterns than others. Finding the right fit between trader, trading method, and market is a key to success.
- **Create a trading business**: Long-term trading success comes from having the correct business structures. For instance, if you trade under a limited company, then you can offset some profits against expenses. Making a profit is one element of running a successful business. The single best predictor of failure is when a trader forgets that this is his or her business. Taking long holidays may be fun, but will these bring you income?

- **Mentorship:** Find a mentor to get it right the first time. Successful performance with new day traders usually comes from the alliance with a mentor. Such a person can help the new trader to set up and start out on the right foot. You learn trading by seeing a mentor's logic and by having that mentor observe your trading. The right mentorship goes a long way toward shortening learning curves.
- **Knowledge, practice, and implementation.** The reality is that success in any field requires dedication to learn the rules of trading, practicing your trades, and implementing strategies that work for you. Once you have developed a strategy, hone it into a finely crafted trading methodology. Remember: if you break your own trading rules and strategies—you will ultimately be drummed out of the business of trading.
- **Start with finding the three M's.** These are the foundation of success, upon which you build skills and experience.

Mentor—Method—Markets

- Now that we've stated the dangers of emotions, let's move on to trading techniques and making money from trading. It can be an enjoyable journey, so let's begin.

Establish Trading Goals and Objectives

As a trader, you need to have strategies in place. The following is a short list of questions for you to consider:

- What cash flow do you need? That is, what do you consider a fair and reasonable salary?
  - Break this down to annual rate of return, monthly, and what you need to achieve daily.
- Do you want to participate with portfolio managers, that is, full time or part time?
- Can you handle the stress of trading every day?
- Do you have the patience for long-term trading?
- What kind of personality do you have?

- Do you need lots of action?
- Do you need to be in control of market orders (make decisions) all the time?
- Can you take advice from a mentor, while you gain experience in trading?
- What trading books have you read?
- Which top traders do you most admire and why?
- Would you copy other traders' style of trading?

Test Your Current Knowledge

The following is a simple test of your trading knowledge. If you get more questions incorrect than makes you feel uncomfortable, go back to the drawing board.

- Is ratio analysis really important? Are such ratios used in isolation or compared year by year?
- Besides Financial Statements, which other pages in the financial report provide a good overview of the company and why?
- By merely studying a Financial Statement, is it possible to determine whether an investment in company is a good investment or not?
- Can a company with profits of US$50m be directly compared to one with US$550m.
- Can market indices give an indication of share price direction?
- Can you directly compare an EPS of 150 cents to that of 790 cents and determine that the latter share is the better investment?
- Define fundamental analysis in your own words.
- Define the shareholders equation.
- Do all investments carry the same risk?
- Do share prices reflect historical trends or only future anticipated events?
- How do you diversify a portfolio?
- Does a share price always reflect the underlying true or intrinsic value, or at some point should reflect this value?
- Does diversification reduce market risk?
- Does investing mean that every one of your decisions will be correct?

- Does the authorized or issued share capital form part of the company balance sheet?
- Does the exchange rate have an impact on company profitability and if so why?
- Expenses are divided into two categories. What are they?
- Explain why analysing shares using their share price is often more useful that using the total size of the company?
- Give an example of quality of earnings.
- Give two rights of shareholders.
- Glancing at the financial statements, is it always apparent that a balance sheet has improved?
- How do you define ratio analysis?
- How are preference shares different from ordinary shares?
- How can Shareholders' equity in a company be defined?
- How do companies raise finance?
- How do interest rates generally affect share prices?
- How do you calculate a company's policy on paying dividends? Where is this detail found?
- How is it that one year a company's share price may trade on a PE of five times, and the next year at 15 times?
- How is risk in assets generally measured? On this measurement is an investment in equities more or less risky than an investment in bonds?
- How is the debt to equity ratio defined and what does this ratio provide a clear indication of?
- In a company, are the shareholders different from the directors?
- Is a shareholder always entitled to a dividend?
- Is market depth a consideration when buying a share?
- Is market volatility seen as an advantage or disadvantage to traders?
- Is the Dow Jones a simple or weighted average?
- Is the Income Statement or the Balance sheet like a financial snapshot in time?
- Is there any importance in the list of shares making new 12-month highs?
- Is the size of a company important to analyse before investing?
- Is trading in shares considered more risky than investing in shares, and if so, why?

- Must shareholders approve a company to buy back its own shares?
- Name three different category types of financial ratios?
- Name at least two books of records that all companies must maintain?
- Name five basic facts about a company that you should know before investing or trading.
- Name the three types of economic system.
- Name two ratios that newspapers quote next to each share price.
- Once issued, is a company able to buy back its own shares? If yes, under what circumstances?
- Over the longer period, which asset class has outperformed all other asset classes, especially on an after tax and inflation basis?
- Over time, has an investment in shares produced a return in excess of the inflation rate?
- Should the role of chairperson and chief executive officer be different?
- State three main advantages in investing into listed shares.
- State three main disadvantages for investing into listed shares.
- Typically, is a higher or a lower stock turn ratio indicative of a more productive company?
- What are three advantages to having a company's shares listed on a stock exchange?
- What are five main points of detail that must be included in a company prospectus?
- What are market indices?
- What are some of the more important information required in the prelisting statement?
- What are the two main purposes and benefits of a stock exchange?
- What are the four main methods of listing a company?
- What are the four fundamental accounting concepts?
- What are the main company specific factors to analyze when assessing a share?
- What are the main components of the annual financial statements?
- What are the most important numbers for an existing long-term investor?
- What are the three main classes of investment in which one can invest?

- What are the three main ingredients of a financial plan for success?
- What are the two activities of capital markets?
- What are the two main liquidity ratios?
- What does EVA stand for and what is the basic premise underlying the use of this ratio in attempting to determine a company's profitability.
- What does macroeconomic factors include?
- What does microeconomic factors include?
- What duty do directors have to the companies that they represent?
- What is a net asset turn ratio and what is its significance?
- What is a net cash outflow or inflow for the year at an operating level?
- What is a percentage increase in margin?
- What is a put option?
- What is a secured corporate bond?
- What is insider dealing?

CHAPTER 4

Strategy

"You get recessions, you have stock market declines. If you don't understand that's going to happen, then you're not ready, you won't do well in the markets."

—Peter Lynch (1944–present), American Businessman and Stock Investor

Trading Penny Stocks

Basic Steps

Steps	
1	You need to decide whether you will trade through a broker of carry out trades via an online brokerage house.
	Remember that in both cases above, the secret is the ability to have extremely fast trade executions.
	Slow trading execution times can result in massive losses due to the fluctuations in the stock price while you wait.
2	Next, you start doing research on companies to potentially invest in.
	This requires in-depth analysis so you can avoid the higher risk stocks and focus on companies with real potential.
	Set up your own criteria to invest. Use a simple seven-point strategy to include buying shares in which companies have stable gross profit margins, have increasing earnings per share (EPS) growth, are in sectors that are on the upswing and not affected by wild changes in price earnings (PE) ratios.
3	Post-acquisition, you need to set up a method to watch the shares. For instance, what is your exit strategy? Do you have stop loss? Remember that trading in penny shares is not a buy-and-hold strategy. Penny stock traders often hold shares for less than a day—or even trading in and out of the shares multiple times per day. You have to be able to dedicate the time to being aware of the fluctuations in the price so you can exit at a profitable moment.

There are two methods to trading penny stocks just as there are with any other stock. The only difference is the small changes in stock price can be huge profits or losses. Things move faster at the penny stock level than they do with shares at $50 each.

Buy and Sell

The aim is to buy at a low price and sell at a higher price.

This strategy is best suited for a method called *Scalping*. This is where traders take a number of positions and aim to make small profits on a consistent basis.

Short and Buy Back

Shorting a share takes courage and even more analysis and research. In this case, you believe that the share will fall and you want to profit from that fall.

When you short a stock you effectively borrow shares from your brokerage firm at the current price. When the share falls, you effectively buy it back and return the stock to the brokerage. A stock starting at $1.25 that you short down to $1 would result in $0.25 profit per share.

With electronic markets, the stock is borrowed from multiple sources.

There is more risk on shorting stocks because the downside is often unpredictable.

Long, Short, and Hedging

Shorting

The strategy on which successful investment decisions are based should be to use whatever is available to you on the exchange of your choice.

Hedge Strategies

A long and short portfolio hedge is run at appropriate times.

Assume that you have a long-term portfolio with COMPANY X.

The portfolio aims to provide you with income in the long term via dividend income. So, effectively, the number of shares in that stock is more important than the share price, as dividends get paid out to you based on the number of share that you hold.

However, if you believe that the Company X share price is going to temporally fall due to an anomaly, then the strategy should be:

- Hedge Company X in your long-term portfolio with a SHORT on company X.
- When the share falls, you close the SHORT position.
- Use the profits from the SHORT position to acquire additional shares in COMPANY X.
- This has had a two-fold benefit:
  - The value of COMPANY X in the portfolio is increased and thus rebalances the long-term portfolio.
  - You have more shares in Company X, so you should get more dividends in future.

Note that hedging positions take constant attention.

One way to take advantage of market movements is to create your own hedge. For instance, you can take the 10 smallest penny shares and the 10 biggest penny shares and hedge the worst against the best.

How do you do it? Take 10 shares with prices of US$5 and 10 with prices of US$1. Buy US$100 in each of the US$5 stocks and SHORT US$100 in the worst stocks.

If the market rises we should start to make losses on the 10 SHORTS, but being the 10 worst shares they should rise a lot less that our top 10 long positions.

What if the market falls? Cut your losses quickly, so tight stop-loss policies must be employed. In fact, the following seems basic and logical, but traders need to be reminded:

Do not invest:

- In any unlisted securities.
- In companies with poor liquidity.
- In Cyclical shares
- In companies undergoing massive restructuring.

It is preferred that you trade shares with sound balance sheets and fairly predictable earnings streams.

CHAPTER 5

Trading Rules

"If stock market experts were so expert, they would be buying stock, not selling advice."

—Norman Ralph Augustine (1935–Present), American
Aerospace Businessman and Under Secretary

Before You Trade

- **Review Market Noise.** Skilled traders follow the correlation of international markets. Essentially, you need to understand how global markets influence the markets you wish to trade in. A suggestion is to look at sector indices and assess how these have reacted to such market noise. Once you have done that, assess how shares within sectors have been influenced. Such analysis can act as warning signals of potential shifts in the overall market and thus specific shares.
- **Determine the market you wish to trade?** Saying that a sector looks interesting is not good enough. You must have software to assess market movements, cyclical nature of sectors, and an influence of shares. One way to determine this is to use a "Market Carpet".
  - A Market Carpet is a schematic representation of the market at-a-glance. Specific stocks are represented as squares that are colored on a green (prices are up) to red (prices are down) spectrum. In this way, market carpets show information at a glance.
- **Establish trading boundaries.** To complete the above rule with a rule: keep three to five times the money in your trading account than is needed for any acquisition. You may have to reduce your

position to comply and also avoid trading decisions based on the amount of money in your account. There will be times when a "hot" tip will convince you to buy a share out of your limits—don't. You will simply be risking your whole portfolio if you do.

- **Build a salary buffer:** You need to build a salary buffer from your profits. So, whatever you expect to earn a month, build a buffer of six months' worth. This will give you the comfort to trade with less pressure.

Trading Specific

- **Determine a portfolio diversification strategy.** If you have decided, after analysis, that you wish to be invested in Finance, Mining, and Property, THEN ALL Industrial shares are eliminated from analysis. If your portfolio or strategy states that you wish to buy three shares, then analyze five shares, because the timing of these shares may not be right for your strategy. I usually select five shares to assess based on fundamentals and then eliminate two based solely on technicals.
- **Confirm one-out-of-three trade.** Of the three trades, as set out in the above rule, I recommend that you choose only one. Remember that the more stocks you have in your portfolio, the more time it takes to assess, reassess, and trade such stocks.
- **Start relatively small.** Start by making virtual trades, before you enter the real world of stockbroking. Then begin to trade in small amounts, such as US$1,000 per share and get five shares.
- **Set up clear BUY and SELL points.** This rule is easy to say and every trader has the intention to keep to this rule, but many fail to do so. Here is the problem: a trader states that he will sell a share if it falls by 10%. When the share does fall by 10%, the trader hesitates and keeps the share, hoping that the share will turnaround.
- **Do you really have to trade today?** Stated differently, if you are not comfortable or your rules don't line up for a trade, then I suggest that you stay out of the market. Another way of stating this rule, you do not have to trade every day, or even hold a position every day. The novice trader often feels that he or she must have

an open position every day—this is not true. There are times when the market is completely dead or too volatile. Use these times to complete research and market analysis. Successful traders tend to have patience and strict discipline, enabling them to effortlessly wait for an opportunity before they acquire securities.

- **Patience is a virtue.** Strangely, not every trade will be a profitable one. An obvious statement to make is that markets do go up, but also fall. My strongest recommendation is to stick to your strategy and to keep within your predetermined chosen markets. Ultimately, you will also learn to wait before acting on a selected Buy or Sell strategy.

- **Emotion can kill you.** Experts always say the same thing: never chase a share or market, even if you intended to acquire a share, but failed to execute your trade on time or at the predetermined price. Remember that there will always be other opportunities. To remove emotion, always have a stop loss and an exit strategy. If the market suddenly moves in the opposite direction of your trade, you need to know that your stop will be executed. As such, there is absolutely no reason to panic.

- **Averaging down or up is a skill.** The rule to averaging is not to add more to a position than you already have. For instance, if you have 100 shares in ABC Limited, don't buy an additional 100 shares in the share price falls. An ideal situation is to pyramid by 50% of the shares, then 25%, followed by 10%. This is conditional on the market showing promising signs of a turnaround. It is also recommended that beginners avoid the "inverted pyramid" type of averaging. This is when you add more than your original position with every new averaging down. This is dangerous, as any market reversal can render you bankrupt.

- **Do you have to trade-specific markets?** It is always recommended that beginner traders develop an understanding of local bourses before they move to trading global exchanges. This does not, however, mean that they negate the importance of trading outside their country. There are times when you should ignore local trends in favor of foreign ones. The expression is that you should trade within your level of comfort.

Actual Trading

- **Stay out of the market for the first 30 minutes of trading.** This rule helps beginners to be patient and to be more careful about the trades before entries are made. Admittedly, this rule means that you will miss some opportunities, but it is better to miss entries than to make bad ones.

- **Avoid market orders.** Placing an order at the current market price is purely a lazy way of trading. The skilled trader will determine liquidity and tradability before putting in an offer. To avoid violating this rule, place specific price limit orders, using the 3-2-1 rule.

- **Stagger pricing.** If you want to get the best price possible for a number of shares, you may want to do it in four instalments. This enables the beginner to see if the market is moving in his or her direction before becoming totally committed. Successful traders use both fundamentals and technical signals to guide their trading and to determine pricing.

- **Cut losses.** When a share falls to your stop loss—sell immediately. If you get into the habit of keeping to your rules, you will ultimately find that trading is less stressful and more analytical. The rule is simple: admit that you made a trading mistake and move onto the next trade. Strangely, you can be a successful trader by being right on less than 50% of your trades. The condition is that you keep to your stop losses, but let your profits run.

- **Let profits run.** There is an old saying that a share can only fall by 100%, but can continue to rise infinitely. So, why would you cut profits short? The reason is that young traders tend to panic when shares rise or fall too quickly. Admittedly, there is no problem in taking profits, but why not let your profits increase to higher levels? Many expert traders concur that you should never take a profit simply for the sake of a profit. You should have a reason to close out a profitable position

- **Sometimes, losses and profits make no sense**. During a conference in 2009, I used an example of a trader who saw shares rise on poor financial results, while the same trader saw a share fall on another company's good results. The poor novice was so confused that he decided that being a dentist was easier. The reason for the above is that a share could fall on good results, if those results were not as good as the market forecast and, conversely, a share could rise if poor results were not as bad as the market expected.

- **What is your stop loss?** This rule is easy to understand and to implement. The only difficulty is in choosing a stop. I recommend a 15% initial stop on a trailing basis. Reduce that to 10% when the share rises by 10% and then to 8% when the share has risen by 15%. In this way, you lock in profits, while not being too tight—which could see you being kicked out of your position too quickly. It is always recommended that you immediately get into the habit of always setting a stop loss. Never trade without one.

- **Never ever ignore your stops.** Once placed, your stop loss stays in. keep to this strategy, as you cannot guess which way the market is going. If you try, and ignore stops, you will without doubt regret your decision.

- **Never add to a losing position**. If a share is falling, there will be a temptation to try and rescue the share by averaging down. Remember that this strategy is very specific and linked to numerous filters. It is not a guessing game as many novice traders believe, to their regret as they merely compound ultimate losses.

- **Can you judge potential profits before you trade?** My personal trading mentor—back some 15 years ago—told me to have a plan in place to sell your security even before you enter a trade. Essentially, it goes like this: if a stock rises by 15%, place on a watch list. If the stock rises by another 10%, sell enough shares to recoup your original cost. I have added the following to my mentor's strategy: when you recoup your original cost, remove the share from your portfolio. Have a second "Free Share" portfolio, which you keep for the long term. Have a stop loss of 15%.

- **Place stops immediately.** This is merely a rule to stress the importance of stops. Never break this rule, under any circumstance as it is the best way to protect your capital.

Post Trades

- **Continuously monitor trades.** There is no point in monitoring long-term trades every day and, conversely, it is plain stupid to monitor short-term trades only every month. In the first instance you are wasting your time, while in the second instance you could end up with a stock falling to nothing. The important point is that you should use short-term technical signals for short-term positions, which includes strategic and pertinent monitoring of your stocks.

- **Should you be flexible with your stop loss strategy?** The simple answer is that you can. For instance, if a position rises really fast, it is recommended that you tighten your stop to lock in profits. Sometimes this change in stop enables the trader to take profit beyond his or her original profit target.

- **Always be flexible, but don't forget to take profits**. The strategy is to know your own timetable. For instance, if you know that you have to be in conference for two days, then sell short positions which you will not be able to monitor.

- **Take regular breaks.** Trading every day does eventually get boring. And boring gets to hamper your judgment. It is suggested that traders take a complete trading break every six weeks. If you are successful, go on holiday for a week, but if you made a loss, spend the next week researching and analysing markets. A break from the trading desk helps you to reassess your strategies and see the market in a fresh manner.

- **Believe in yourself.** Once a strategy has been established, don't let colleagues or rumors deter you from trading to your plan. Decisions made during the trading day based upon short-term shifting trends or news items are often disastrous. It is better to formulate a strategy based on logic before the market opens, then enter the market at a predetermined price range.

- **Stay the course.** Remember that you have to be strong willed and disciplined to succeed in the market. Stick to your strategy and you will dramatically increase the probability of trading profits over losses.

- **Analyze every trade.** Every time I trade, I write down the time, date, and price of the trade. I also provide a reason for the trade. Every week, look at the successes and failures of your trades and critically assess why you bought and sold the stocks. Over time, you will develop an eye for profitable situations and a logic for selling. Personally, I analyze every trade, even after two decades of active trading.

The above trading rules are important and will take time for novice traders to start implementing them. Somehow, novice traders often find it difficult to incorporate these rules into their daily trading plans. As such, I have no doubt that it will take time for you to do so, but be warned: the longer it takes you to start using these rules, the quicker you are headed for losses.

CHAPTER 6

Combining Fundamental and Technical Analysis

"Rule no 1: never lose money. Rule no 2: never forget rule no 1."
—Warren Buffett (1930–Present), American Investor

The Relationship Between EPS, PE, and Share Price

How Do These Variables Influence Share Price?

Well, let's start with the breakdown of how an earnings per share (EPS) is derived. In a company's Income Statement the Attributable profit is divided by the number of shares in issue to calculate the EPS.

So now we have two variables that could influence the EPS, namely the derived profit attributable to shares holders and the number of shares in issue. This means that a trader needs to understand the number of variables that will influence attributable profit, such as interest paid and taxes. If a company has a high debt level and interest rates are raised, profits will fall as higher interest is paid.

Thus, less profits paid means lower EPS if shares issued remain unchanged.

Now, if additional shares are issued during the year, then EPS also falls; profits divided by a higher number of shares in issue equates to a lower EPS.

Note, the formula for Share Price is: Price Earnings multiplied by EPS.

So, if PE = SHARE PRICE DIVIDED BY EPS, then we can surmise that a lower EPS will result in a higher price earnings (PE) ratio. This means that the share has become more expensive. Alternatively, you can change the formula to SHARE PRICE = PE MULTIPLIED BY EPS

Now, if you use a basic valuation methodology to forecast EPS in the next 12 months, you can determine whether a share price today is over- or undervalued.

EXAMPLE:

- Current share price is US$13.00
- Latest EPS is 100c
- The company has a 10 percent annual EPS growth
- Current PE is 15 times
- The average PE for the past three years is 12 times.

What is the current fair value and can you calculate a basic 12 month forecast.

Aim	Calculation	Answer
FAIR VALUE	SP = PE × EPS	US$15.00
12 MONTH FORECAST	SP = Current PE × FORECAST EPS SP = Ave PE × FORECAST EPS	Between US$13.20 and US$16.50

CONCLUSION:
- The company's share price is US$15 compared to a current price of US$13, which means that there is a possible upside of 15.4 percent. A POTENTIAL SHORT-TERM TRADE.
- Compared to the next 12 months, the share could rise from US$13 to between US$13.20 and US$16.50. THIS IS A POTENTIAL 1.5 percent to 26 percent. THE DISCREPANCY IS TOO VAST AND THUS NOT A LONG-TERM OPPORTUNITY.

The Fundamental Perspective

The primary purpose of fundamental analysis is to correctly understand and provide logical reasons for buying or selling a share, that is, it provides the foundation for logical decision making before you trade. In fact, fundamentals provide traders with the analytical tools to understand the underlying value of securities and to determine whether such securities are under- or overvalued. Imagine selling a share when it hit a technical indicator SELL point, only to discover that the company is about to merger with a multinational and the share price quadruples?

Fundamental analysis should be applied to all investments, whether in the equity market, gilts, or derivatives. There is always a need to apply sound analysis to wider markets through economic and business analysis and investment strategy.

Simply stated, look at political, economic, business, and technological variables to conclude whether a company or specific security will be influenced or not and whether, in fact, it is worth buying at all.

What Is Technical Analysis?

Quite simply, technical analysis is the study of the history of combined investor and trader buy and sell sentiment and behavior and its potential effect on the current and expected future price of securities. In essence, the information to conduct technical analysis is derived using trading software packages, which use price histories and financial ratios and statements, together with time and volume statistics. These variables enable traders to use these technical program to form graphs which they use to forecast trends and price action.

Technical Analysis versus Fundamental Analysis

Fundamentalists believe that the value of securities is best assessed by investigating complex financial statements, quality of directors and key management and specially earnings and growth rates. They follow intricate patterns of analysis to make forecasts on securities in line with global markets and often relative to economic cycles.

Today, many analysts concentrate on company fundamentals, monitoring company trends and assessing how these could influence investors' and traders' perception of current and future share prices. This behavior is collectively called market or investor sentiment.

Example: In the late 1990s while working at stockbrokers Global Capital Securities as Head of Research, I found my analysis on a motor-based company peculiar and I started to doubt myself. This company's turnover had increased from ZAR1 billion to ZAR3 billion within a three year period and profits had more than doubled. Yet the share price stayed at the 300 cent level during this entire period.

How could that happen?

Further and more in-depth analysis highlighted that investors simply did not trust management or the figures in the financials. Market sentiment was negative and a higher share price was not going to happen.

Therefore, while fundamental analysis highlights crucial corporate trends and technical analysis identifies trend patterns, investor sentiment holds the key to whether prices will actually move.

This book adopts the stance that fundamental and technical analysis are mutually inclusive. In fact, these two systems can be used in reverse. Traders can use technical analysis to identify securities with potential positive trends and then use fundamental analysis to filter out those that do not meet your predetermined strategies. If more traders used both systems to determine what and when to buy or sell securities, many would be more successful.

Basic fundamental analytical concepts were covered in the previous chapter. Now, let's do the same for technicals, which can be applied as follows:

Tools

- A filter tool to identify potential investments.
- A timing tool to determine more accurately timed entry and exit points.

Questions

- What is the current share price trend?
- When did this trend start?

- When did this trend last change?
- What are the major support and resistance levels?
- Where is the share positioned relative to these major support and resistance levels?
- Does the overall market support this trend?
- Have there been any important reversal patterns?
- Have you drafted a three point moving average, using 9, 21 and 200 day moving averages?
- Identify the share price relative to its moving averages?
- Is the share in a strong sector relative to the overall market?
- Are momentum indicators positive or negative?
- Do they confirm the stock's current movement?
- Does the share display strong volume movement?
- Does recent share movement confirm the current trend or does it indicate a likely trend change?
- By answering the above questions, traders will filter out shares that are weak, so that they can concentrate on those that offer potential.

Checklist for Novice Traders

- **Trends and trading ranges**: This is the easiest technical indicator and is a line drawn on a share graph that touches and meets at least three points. If prices are generally rising, then the general trend is up. Uptrends defined as both the low and high points being higher each day.

- Penny shares tend to move in trends only 30 percent of the time, while mostly they move in a sideways band, also called a trading range.

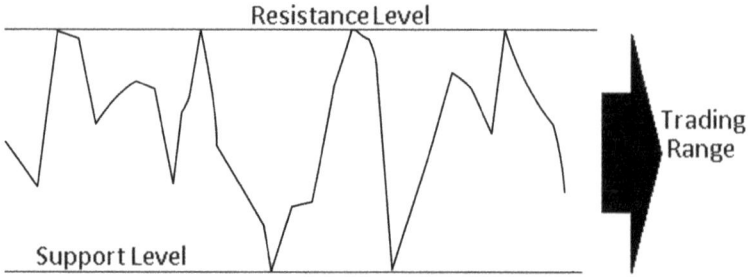

- **Support and Resistance**: In the above diagram two lines are drawn. The first touches three points above the share graph and the second three point below the share price. The top line represents a resistance level, which means that the share touches that point and falls. The bottom line represents a support level.
- **Moving Averages**: Also called simply price averages, these are average prices over a defined period of time. The norm is to use three averages in a graph, such as 9, 21 and 200 days. They are used to forecast changes in investor sentiment as prices move above or below the averages.

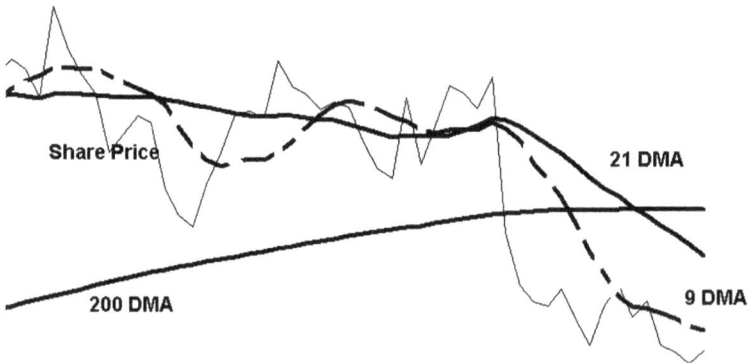

- **Volume and Momentum**: These two indicators confirm that a trend is strong and highlights whether the number of days when prices are falling outnumber (or not) days when the share is rising. This is identified as the share's momentum. If either indictors start to rise, traders can assume that the trend is strengthening.

- **Simple Relative Performance**: This simple method is used to determine how a sector or share is performing relative to another sector or share. For instance, if you want to determine whether the US Dow Jones outperforms the London Stock Exchange FT 100, you would divide one Index by another. If the ratio is going up, then the stock/Sector/Index is outperforming the market or company. The alternative is if the ratio is going down, then stock is weakening relative to its competitor or market.

DOW JONES VERSES FT-100

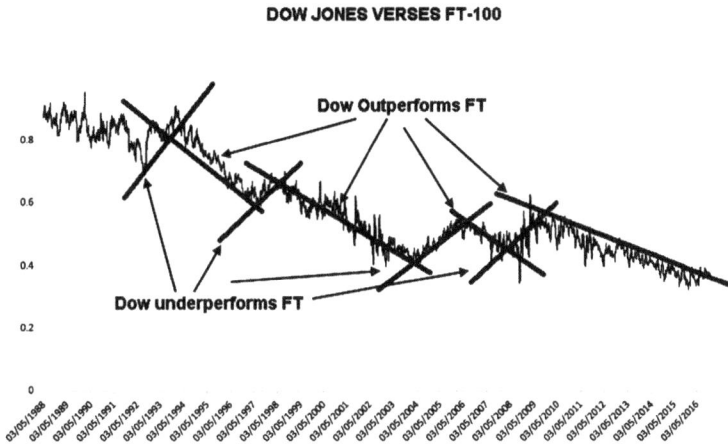

Identifying Growth Sectors

When trading penny shares, it is important to at the outset to determine which sectors you are going to trade. Therefore, you need to develop a Filter that enables you to remove weak shares and Indices from your analysis. As such, the main thrust of the Filter -is to identify sectors or Indices that have higher potential growth when compared to other Indices. For instance, why would you trade mining shares if the sector indicators highlight that the market is sluggish, or in a downward trend?

The aim is therefore to first select sectors by identifying indices that are showing positive growth.

The first question that must be asked, therefore, is what are traders buying? The second question: are there enough traders active in these sectors to move share prices? The third question is to ask how do you find what traders' sentiment is toward shares?

One method is to identify sectors that are on the upswing by looking at volume growth in the Indices. Remember that not all shares in a sector form part of the Indices. So, be aware that such trading immediately eliminates smaller and thus higher risk shares within these sectors, which effectively means that you are eliminating the penny shares that you have set out to trade.. The first filter is thus to identify which Indices have the highest volume growth. The second is to identify the penny shares within these high volume growth shares that meet your trading strategy.

Volume-based Technical Analysis

Identifying how traders and investors view securities and Indices is called sentiment analysis. Such sentiment indicators are not easy to use as they tend to be developed by global stockbrokers for their clients, so they have a specific purpose which may not meet your specific penny share trading strategies. The essence of these indicators is to assess and quantify whether the overall market sentiment is optimistic or pessimistic. After some research, I found a number of indicators that can be used to highlight investor sentiment and thus Index growth.

These include economic variables (money flow and supply/demand balances) and technical indicators (Chaikin money flow). I prefer more simplistic volume-related indicators, which highlights three target areas for penny share traders:

- Money flow Identifier
- Volume of net trades
- Volume surge Identifier
- **Money flow Identifie**r: Simplistic, but effective and used to determine whether there are more buyers than sellers trading a specific share.
- **SBV Oscillator (Selling & Buying Volume):** It is used to highlight Bullish or Bearish money flows. Essentially, it is used to determine whether a trend will change from positive to negative or vice versa.
- Money Flow Index (MFI): This momentum indicator uses volume and high, low, and close prices into the calculation to determine and measure buying and selling pressure.

These indicators give traders a sense of the strength of trading volume. Remember that penny shares often have poor traded volume, which makes it difficult to implement exit strategies.

Therefore, if the MFI is up, money is leaving the share and the share will fall.

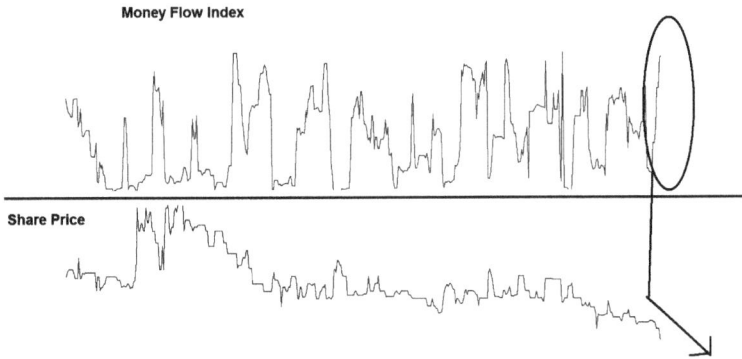

Alternative Indicators

Volume:

- **Net trades**: Bullish and bearish volume accumulation can also be assessed by analysing volume. This indicator is also called Bearish and bullish volume accumulations, and is used to assess how strongly net buyers over sellers are and how this can influence stock, index, or overall market.
- **Surge Identifier**: When markets and sectors are dominated by few organisations and institutions, it is important to use an indicator to determine if there will be a massive buy or sell order from such organisations that could signal major price movements.

Indices—Identifying Trend Indicators

Indicator 1: The Advance-Decline Line

Indicator 1	
Name	The Advance-Decline Line
Type of indicator	A market breadth indicator
Calculation	Daily or weekly data
Aim	Define general market action
Trader perspective	Watch for divergences

If the Overall Index (on any stock exchange) and Indicator 1 are moving in the same direction, traders can assume that the current trend will continue. However, if the Index and Indicator move in different directions, a warning trigger is issued.

The reason for advocating Indicator 1 is that it is easy to use, particularly when trading penny shares. In essence, this indicator is created and maintained by you, as all you have to do is calculate the net difference between increases and declines and then adding the net amount to an index; which you make up.

For example, if you decide on an index number of 10000 and the net difference between buyers and sellers today is a number of 510 (buyers are 990 and sellers 480 = 510), then your index has risen to 10510. Continue to do that daily and quickly you establish your own Indicator 1.

Indicator 2: Upside-Downside Volume Ratio

Indicator 2	
Name	Upside-Downside Volume Ratio
Type of indicator	Market breadth indicator
Calculation	Divide volume of increasing issues by volume of declining issues. Daily or weekly data is used
Aim	Determine overbought/oversold positions
Trader perspective	The indicator provides Traders with an understanding as to whether a stock has momentum

This technical indicator highlights the relationship between the volumes of rising and declining shares on an exchange. Effectively, this ratio is used to assess the momentum of the market at any predetermined time.

The ratio is calculated by dividing the number of shares that have risen by those that have fallen; as follows:

Issue	Calculation
Rising Issues	Total volume traded of shares that closed above their opening price
Falling Issues	Total volume traded of securities that closed below their opening price

Insignificant movements are smoothed using a standard moving average, which results in the equation being equal to values above and below 1.

Values	Results in terms of Volume
Greater than 1	Generated when more issues are rising than declining.
Less than 1	Created when more issues are declining than advancing.

The upside/downside ratio is very effective in gauging market conditions that are either overbought or undersold. Low values can indicate that the market is becoming oversold and high value can demonstrate that the market is becoming overbought.

Share Selection Filter

The following may seem too simplistic. However, the aim is to move rapidly through a host of companies to see which you have picked to conduct proper analysis and technical assessments.

The way that traders can do this is via a filter to set the parameters according to their specific strategies. This includes market cap, price range, liquidity/tradability, earnings growth, and strength of financials—ratio analysis

Step 1: Market Cap

- Decide on the size of company you wish to invest in. Remember that the larger the company is, the less the risk associated to trading that stock.
- The size of the company (in money terms) is calculated by multiplying the number of shares in issue with the company's share price. This is called the company's Market Capitalization.
- If you choose a figure that is too high, you will have too few companies to select. The aim is to look at companies within a market cap range. For example, Trader A wishes to select at companies with a market cap of between US$500 million and US$1 billion.

- If you move your parameter up, the companies become larger and less risky.
- If you move the parameter down, the companies become smaller and more risky.

Step 2: Share Price

- Now that you have selected a range of companies according to market cap, you need to decide how much you are willing to spend per share. This means that if you want to buy shares in US$100,000 lots and you want 10 share in your portfolio, you will need US$1 million to trade.
- If you don't have that amount of cash, reduce the amount of cash you wish to spend per share. This enables you to reduce the selected shares (Step 1) by looking for at price per share.
- At this point, you have not even looked at the strength of the company.

Step 3: Liquidity/Tradability

- There is no point in selecting companies to trade if these shares do not trade.
- The average number of share that needs to be traded per week is at least 400,000 shares. Any less, and the company does not have enough free shares to trade.
- Your ability to exit a position is as important as being able to buy a share

Step 4: Earnings Growth

- Always buy shares in companies that have positive earnings per share growth.
- Decide on the growth (in percentage terms) that will make you feel comfortable and filter out shares that don't meet that criteria.
- The norm is to immediately eliminate all shares that will show growth that is less than the money market rate. This rate is also called the risk free rate. For instance, if you can invest your money

in the money market at 4 percent a year interest, why would you invest in shares that have less growth?

Now: you have selected shares from growth Indices. You have filtered these down according to your risk profile (size of company), then you looked at the price of the company and removed those companies that are too expensive. After that, you eliminated illiquid stocks and those that have low profit rates.

Now comes the section that is a little more difficult, but remember that you have reduced every hundred shares down to a possible six shares. This is the rate at which your filter should work and you have yet to conduct any analysis.

Step 5 is the use of ratios to eliminate—or determine strength—of the remaining stocks in your filter.

Step 5: Strength of Financials—Ratio Analysis

There is a lot to be said for finding a company's true value; it is not an easy task and is definitely subjective. If you have yet to discover this wisdom, then look at, for instance, the entrepreneur who wishes to sell his company, compared to the potential buyer. Naturally, while the seller will want to secure the highest price, the buyer will want to pay as little as possible.

Therefore, the value of the company is ultimately the worth that both parties will consider to be **fair and realistic.** The only manner to achieve this is for the owner to prove to the buyer that the company is financially sound, nonfinancial aspects (goodwill and other intangibles) are entrenched and the future profitability of his company is not in question.

While financial aspects can be assessed, the future potential needs to be conveyed in a manner that convinces the buyer that the price is fair and realistic.

- I have a computerized system to conduct ratio analysis rapidly; send me a request on jacques@bci.za.com for a copy.
- Get hold of a company's annual results, either the hard copy or the electronic version. All companies have websites from which you can access annual reports.

- The following filter is simple. If a company's ratios do not meet industry norms, stop the analysis.
- These norms do differ between industries. If you want a copy of current industry norms, contact me on jacques@bci.za.com.

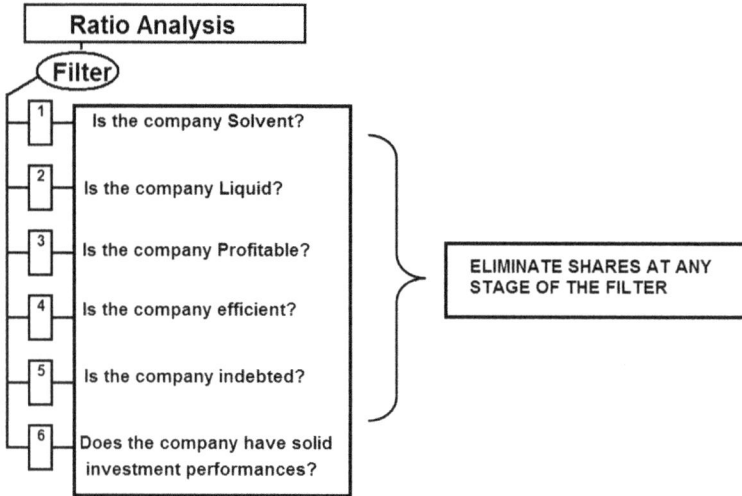

```
┌─────────────────────────┐
│     Ratio Analysis      │
└─────────────────────────┘
  ╭────────╮
  │ Filter │
  ╰────────╯
   ┌───┐
   │ 1 │── Is the company Solvent?
   └───┘                              ╲
   ┌───┐                               ╲
   │ 2 │── Is the company Liquid?       ╲
   └───┘                                 ╲
   ┌───┐                                  ┌───────────────────────┐
   │ 3 │── Is the company Profitable?     │ ELIMINATE SHARES AT ANY│
   └───┘                                  │ STAGE OF THE FILTER    │
   ┌───┐                                  └───────────────────────┘
   │ 4 │── Is the company efficient?    ╱
   └───┘                                 ╱
   ┌───┐                                ╱
   │ 5 │── Is the company indebted?    ╱
   └───┘
   ┌───┐
   │ 6 │── Does the company have solid
   └───┘   investment performances?
```

Area	Ratios Used
Solvency	• General solvency check
Liquidity	• Current asset ratio • Quick ratio (Acid test) • Stock to working capital ratio • Defensive interval ratio
Profitability	• Profit margins • Return on shareholders' equity • Return on net assets • Return on capital employed
Efficiency	• Stock turn • Accounts receivable days • Accounts payable days
Gearing	• Debt:equity (gearing) • Proportional debt ratio • Ordinary shareholders' interest • Long-term debt to capital employed • Interest cover • Gross cash flow to total debt ratio

Investment Performance Ratios	• Earnings per share • Dividend per share • Dividend cover • Earnings yield • Dividend yield • Price to earnings ratio

See Appendix for full calculations.

Step 6: Find True Value

The following offers traders a technique to be ahead of other traders, by building a valuation database that is different to other traders. The system enables you to assess the value of a listed company's assets to effectively attempt to recalculate its listed share price.

Four Elements

Elements	Reasons
Listed divisions	The holding company's listed entities are valued at current market share prices.
Unlisted divisions	These are valued on a PE basis, which takes into account future potential earnings of the firm.
Other	The value of the company's net cash to debt is calculated.
Fully diluted share capital	For conservative estimates, the net worth per share is based on the full number of ordinary shares, N shares, preference shares, and debentures issued.

Method of Calculation

Calculation of the holding company's net worth	
Step 1	Value the listed entities
Step 2	Value the unlisted entities (p:e ratios)
Step 3	Value the net other (cash, debt, and working capital)
Step 4: add 1, 2, & 3	**Total recalculated value of holding company**

Calculation of the holding company's premium/discount rating	
Step 1	Calculate full shares in issue
Step 2	Net worth × shares in issue
Step 3: Total worth per share	NET WORTH PER SHARE
Step 4: Premium/discount rating	Holding company share price ÷ Net worth per share

The company's share price divided by the recalculated net worth provides a discount (if negative) or premium (if positive) rating. This discount/premium rating must be data-based daily, so as to provide a means to assess whether a rating is the norm in the short to long term.

This provides the investor with **a timing mechanism to buy or sell the share.**

The following fictitious example relates to COMPANY X Ltd, which is a company that offers solid future prospects for investors.

EXAMPLE:

Net Worth Calculation of Company X Ltd	
A Net Worth Calculation! (1 + 2 +3) + 4]	US$ 56.17
B Share Price (live)	US$ 32.00
C Premium/(Discount) [(B + A) expressed as %] (%)	(43.03)

1. COMPANY X Ltd Listed Investments							
Listed divisions	Listed entities' issued share capital	Shares held		Actual price of listed entity	% of Value	Net total	Worth value of entity
	million	%	million	US$	US$	%	$/ share
Zennin Inc.	500	75.00	375	12.00	4 500	45.8	25.7
Duo retail	200	10.00	20	5.00	100	1.0	0.6
Total listed	-	-	-	-	4 600	46.8	26.3

2. COMPANY X Ltd: Unlisted Investments

Unlisted investments	% Held	Division's total earnings (US$m)	Division's attributable earnings (US$m)	Estimated PE (times)	Estimated value (US$m)	% of Total	Net worth value of entity ($/share)
FC Finance	100	200	140	20	2 800	28.5	16.0
J Enterprise	50	120	84	35	2 940	29.9	16.8
Total unlisted					5 740	58.4	32.8

3. COMPANY X Ltd: Other Investments (Net cash to debt position)			
	Estimated value (US$m)	% of Total	Net worth value of entity ($/share)
Debt (net of cash)	−110	−1.4	−0.78
Net other working capital	−400	−4.1	−2.3
Total	−510	−5.2	−2.9

4. COMPANY X Ltd: Share Capital	
1. Ordinary shares in issue	100 000 000
2. Preference shares	50 000 000
3. N-Shares	25 000 000
Total shares in issue	175 000 000
Value of Company X Ltd	
Total [1 + 2 + 3]	$9 830 million
Per Share [(1 + 2 + 3) ÷ 4]	$56.17

Conclusion:

- COMPANY X Ltd has a current share price of $32, but a recalculated net worth of $56.17, which means that the company's share is trading at a 43.03 percent discount to its true worth.
- In calculating its true worth, current updated market values for its listed entities were used, while a realistic PE ratio for unlisted divisions was assessed and used to calculate net worth.
- **The net worth** was thus as follows:

1. Listed investments	$4 600 million
2. Unlisted investments	$5 740 million ($510 million)
3. Other investments, net cash to debt position	
TOTAL VALUE (addition of 1,2, & 3)	$9 830 million

Calculation of premium/discount was thus:

1. Total value	$9 830 million
2. Total issued share capital	175 million
3. Total value per share (1 + 2)	$56.17
Premium/discount rating (share price 3 ÷ share price of $32) (43.03%)	

The model also identified that the unlisted entities represent $32.80 of the net worth of International Finance Ltd. This is slightly more than the value of COMPANY X Ltd share price.

The model has thus identified two important areas for the investor.

- A purchase of the share could represent a possible profit percentage of 43.03 percent in the long term.
- There is a possibility that the unlisted entities-which are worth almost as much as the value of the entire company per share— could be sold off.

Testing for Market Volatility

The final step is to ask: Is the market stable enough to invest now, or should I wait? Bollinger bands are used to measure a market's volatility, as this tool warns traders as to whether the market is sluggish or fast paced.

- **Sluggish:** bands contract
- **Fast Pace:** bands expand.

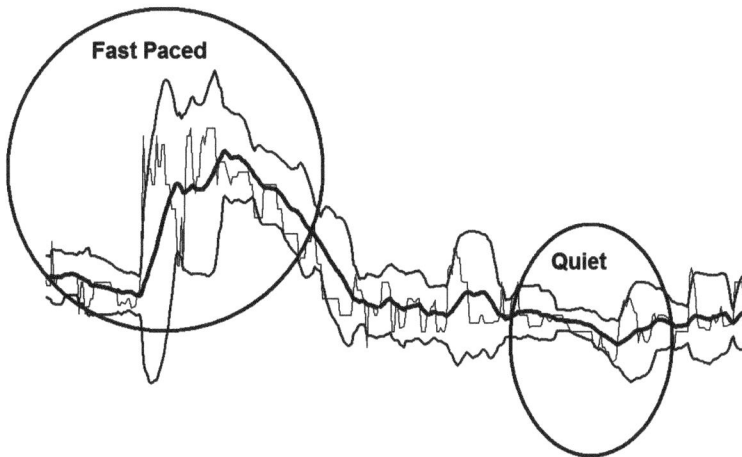

Invest when the market is fast and stay out when the market is slow!

.

CHAPTER 7

Timing Your Trades

"The stock market is filled with individuals who know the price of everything, but the value of nothing."
—Phillip Fisher (1907–2004), American Stock Investor best known
as the Author of Common Stocks and Uncommon Profits

Three Steps to Timing

THREE STEPS TO TIMING YOUR TRADE

Step 1: ➡ Determine The Share's Current Strength

Step 2: ➡ Determine The Share's Trend

Step 3: ➡ Determine The Potential Future Price Strength of the Share

Step 1: Determine Strength of a Share

The easiest indicator to determine current strength is Average Directional Index (ADX), which is easy to use as it is an oscillator that fluctuates between 0 and 100. If the reading is less than 20, the graph signals the trend is weak and if greater than 50 signals the trend is strong.

Note that the ADX is an oscillator, but does not warn of trend that are bullish or bearish. I prefer this indicator—as a first step—to highlight the strength of the trend as it is easy to interpret as it only measures the strength of the current trend.

Step 2: Determine the Share's Trend

Now that you have set out and found the share's current strength, you want to know whether the company's share will continue on that path, that is, will the company's trend continue? Is it strong enough to continue?

To identify whether this is the case with the chosen trade, use the Stochastic Oscillator to indicate whether the share is overbought, oversold, or not. This indictor in effect compares today's price to a preset window of high and low prices to create a range between 0 and 100.

- When the Stochastic lines are above 80, it means the market is overbought.
- When the Stochastic lines are below 20, it means that the market is oversold.

As a rule of thumb, traders should buy when the market is oversold, and sell when the market is overbought.

Step 3: Determine the Potential Future Price Strength of the Share

This is a seldom used indicator, and one that is not included in many software packages. It is, however, one that can be of great assistance to traders. The Ichimoku Kinko Hyo (IKH) is an indicator that traders use to assess possible future price momentum with forecast support and resistance levels.

The following is a basic explanation of IKH, but if you are interested in knowing more about this form of technical analysis, send me a request on jacques@bci.za.com. The Japanese words *Ichimoku Kinko Hyo* tell it all, meaning "one glance cloud chart." It consists of five lines, as follows:

- The standard line
- The turning line
- The delayed line
- The first preceding span
- The second preceding span

While the IKH is brilliant to identify potential future price movements, it is extremely difficult to keep the information updated for the many shares you have placed in a watch list.

Therefore, a traditional moving average technical indicator and the IKH standard/turning lines will give a similar result. As discussed, a buy signal is triggered when the shorter term Moving Average (MA) crosses the longer term MA going upwards. A sell signals is triggered when the opposite takes place.

The above triggers also apply to IKH when quantifying market expectation over a specified time period.

CHAPTER 8

Entry and Exit Points

"Every once in a while, the market does something so stupid it takes your breath away."

—Jim Cramer (1955–Present),
American hedge fund manager.

The 3-2-1 Method

One of the most asked questions in trading is about pricing of shares. Do you buy securities *at market,* or do you try and get these at a discount to the current market value?

In a highly volatile and rapidly changing securities market, the answer is entirely up to you, your strategies and your investment timeframe. The norm is that, the longer your trading timeframe is, the more time you have to buy the share. Conversely, the shorter your trading timeframe is, the quicker you want to get the stock.

My personal philosophy is:

- **Short-term trades:** Buy at a premium. If you need to get the stock NOW, a market order will just place you at the end of the electronic trading execution queue. By the time you get the stock, the price will have moved and you will have lost the deal. This is especially true in geared markets.
- **Long-term traders**: Use the 3-2-1 strategy, as follows:
  ○ For the first three days: place your offer at a discount of 6% to market.
  ○ If your offer has not been take up, change your offer to 2% discount top market for the next two days.

- After this timeframe, change your offer to at market—for one day only.
- If—after this time period—you still haven't being able to get the stock, move the offer to a 2% premium.

Exit Strategies

Always have a stop loss or a trailing stop loss.

A stop loss is simply a level; at which you feel comfortable in selling the share if it fall. So, if you think 10% is an acceptable loss, sell the security if it falls to this level. A trailing stop loss is the same strategy as the stop loss, except that the fall is based on the shares' upward movement. Example:

- Trader buys a share at 100 cents.
- He believes that a 10% loss is acceptable.
- The stop loss is thus 90 cents.
- Assume that the share rise to 130 cents.
- A stop loss would be triggered if the share fell from 130 cents to 90 cents.
- A trailing stop loss would be triggered if the share fell to 117 cents (10% of 130 cents).

Two strategies are important to note:

- The stop loss exit points have to be determined before you get into a trade.
- If the trailing stop loss is triggered, but your overall portfolio is still only marginally affected, consider holding the stock until it hits the stop loss.

CHAPTER 9

The Penny Share Scalper

"Know what you own, and know why you own it."
—Peter Lynch (1944–Present)
US Investor, Mutual Fund Manager and Philanthropist

Let's Define Scalping

The aim of scalp trading is to make a continuous stream of small profits throughout the day. The strategy is deemed successful if you are able to make small profits with less risk per trade. Because of making many trades, it becomes difficult to monitor all positions, so the advice is to have a tight stop loss on each position.

However, this form of trading does require strict discipline and focus, which can make a trading day tense. So, if you cannot concentrate on many trades, spread across global exchanges, then scalping is not for you.

Scalping is thus fast, exciting, and requires an ability to make decisions without hesitation. My recommendation is to use scalping to profit from anomalies in price and a company's true value. So, before you even begin to scalp, research which sectors on global markets are at their most volatile. Ask: what's happening in the world economies? Then look at correlations between shares, sectors, and general markets. Once you've done this, check daily charts to identify resistance levels.

Remember that you are looking for opportunities with low risk and high earning potential.

Forms of Scalping

- **Market related:** Scalpers use futures to capitalize on the difference between a share's opening and closing prices, called a spread. They simultaneously make a bid and an offer on stocks that have major daily trading volumes. This kind of scalping is difficult as profits are generally small.
- **Traditional**:
  - Trader uses price movements to buy large number of highly liquid shares and sells these on small price movements.
  - Trader uses technical indicators to strategize on Entry and Exit levels.

Checklist

Before scalping, check the following:

	Completed	
Checklist	Yes	No
Assess yesterday's price highs and lows		
Assess today's highs and lows?		
Assess the share's 12 month high?		
Assess the share's 12 month low?		
Is there a *Gap*		
What's the difference between the current price and fair value?		

If the objective of scalping is to trade in and out quickly, are there strategies? Do you, in fact, actually need strategies?

A choice is to trade market gaps or breakouts. Experts suggest that such trading is difficult and requires absolutely perfect timing. There is a substantial risk to being long or going short too quickly and, therefore, you risk the possibility of the trend not being as substantial as you expected. In fact, what if the trend turns against you at the very start of a trend? One strategy is to offset this risk by having a two-stage approach to acquiring stocks: Scalp only 50% of your intended funds and the remainder when the trend is confirmed.

As part of your trading journal and strategy objectives, use the following:

- **Realistic Objectives:** Achieve regular small profits on small price fluctuations.
- **Set a Trading Timeframe**: Trade an average of seven to 10 times a day, but never more than 12 times and a minimum of three times. Hold positions for at least two hours, but a maximum of six hours.
- **Trade Execution**: only trade in electronic markets with live share pricing displays.
- **Uncapped Network Connections**: Investigate and get the fastest and most efficient internet system available anywhere in the world.
- **Continuous Research**: After hours and specifically before markets open, I will prepare by undertaking market research so that my trading decisions are with sufficient knowledge. I will always analyze key drivers that may prevent a stock from moving, staying neutral, or rapidly rising or falling.
- **Churning and chasing is forbidden**: My stock choices will be based on my research and experience and I will not chase the market or conduct popular trades.
- **Exit positions**: As scalping is quick, I will not hold overnight positions. Before the end of the day, I will take profits or losses.

True scalpers exit positions quickly if the market doesn't go their way. Don't hold on to a losing position hoping it turns around!

Example of a Scalper

Jackson is a successful day trader, who over the years learned incredibly important lessons which he calls his *"survival bible."*

The following is his personal strategy:

- He will trade only JSE-listed stocks.
- He needs a cash flow of ZAR80,000.00 a month as a "salary."
- He concentrates on penny shares valued at below ZAR10.00 a share.
- He will open four positions every day.
- Each position will be worth ZAR5,000.00 each, that is, he is willing to trade ZAR20,000.00 per day.
- He will close those positions every day, that is, *never go overnight with an open position.*
- He will trade penny shares, but Futures positions, as follows:
  ○ Two positions will be high risk: gearing of 25 times.
  ○ Two positions will be low risk: gearing of 5 times
- He will place an extremely low Stop Loss on the high risk trades, that is, he expects to break even on those trades.
- He will place a 15% stop loss on the low-risk trades.
- He will only trade 50% of the month.
- He will enter trades based on technical analysis and fair value assessment.
- He will trade only during the first 2.5 hours of the day's trading on the JSE.
- He will base his trades on international correlation of markets.

What does the above actually mean?

Firstly, Jackson needs ZAR80,000.00 a month, but he doesn't expect to make that amount in one trade. He is averaging that income over four weeks, which means that he expects to make ZAR20,000.00 a week, or between ZAR2,000.00 and ZAR3,000.00 a day.

Jackson has learned valuable lessons during his early years. He knows that trading conditions are not always conducive to trading, so his first question every day is not "What should I trade today?"

His first question is "Should I trade today?"

Next, Jackson knows that high-risk trading can wipe out your entire profits, so he has a tight stop loss and expects that these two positions to break even. So, he trades 50% of the month and expects 50% of his trades to succeed. Then, he trades the futures positions on international correlation of market movements—what does this mean?

Here is the theory:

- International stock markets influence each other, so the U.S. markets should create optimism in other markets if it is in an upswing.
- Always ensure that a trend is effective with a confirming upswing in a second stock market. For instance, if the U.S. markets are up and the Asian markets follow that trend, then the African markets should follow suit.
- Except that, while the above is accurate, it needs to be honed down further.
  - For instance, if the United States and Asian markets are in an upswing, the JSE should follow.
  - However, the influence of these markets will be effective UNTIL the European markets open.
  - Thus, Jackson trades only the first 2.5 hours of the JSE opening.
  - Other traders suggest the following:
    - Between the JSE opening and 11:30: Correlation of United States and Asian markets influence is 80 percent.
    - Between 11:30 and 14:00: trade market anomalies and noise. Not only are the European markets open, but the local news starts to influence the direction of the JSE.
    - Between 14:00 and the closing of the JSE for the day: U.S. markets have opened and offer new correlation between Europe and the United States.
  - In addition, Jackson looks at three indices in the major markets:
    - **U.S. markets:** Dow Jones Industrial Index, the Nasdaq and the SP500.
    - **Asian markets:** The Shanghai Index, the Hang Send and the Nikkei.
    - **European markets:** Cac40, Dax, and FT100.
  - Effectively, Jackson states the following:
    - If two or more of the above indices are up and confirmed, he will long the previous day's closing WORST performing penny shares.

- If two or more of the above indices are down and confirmed, he will go SHORT on the previous day's closing BEST performing penny shares.

Let's assess Jackson's earnings:

- Four positions per day.
  - Two positions are expected to break even: ZAR0.00
  - Two positions are expected to earn ZAR2,000.00.
    - ZAR2.000,00 for 10 days a month: ZAR20,000.00
    - Earnings on a gearing of five times : ZAR100,000.00
    - Earnings After tax: between ZAR75,000.00 and ZAR80,000.00

Conclusions

- Scalping penny shares can be profitable for traders who are discerning, are disciplined, and base their trades on a combination of fundamentals and technical indicators.
- As a main or a primary strategy scalping can be lucrative. Remember that Jackson expects to break even on his high-risk trading. In fact, on more than one occasion Jackson's strategy has paid off (see below).
- The main lessons learned from scalping penny shares are:
  - Risk is limited when:
    - Trading more securities in lesser amounts takes place.
    - The trading timeframe is limited to a specific period as this reduces the probability of market noise affecting the position.
  - It is easier to trade small amounts of penny shares than trying to buy large amounts of Blue Chips.
  - Penny shares are cheaper and it is easier to earn 20% per trade. For instance, a ZAR10 stock can move to ZAR12 quicker than a ZAR100 moves to ZAR120.

In recent years, Jackson has been able to succeed at least once a month on those extremely high-risk strategies. His most successful trade was as follows:

- Enter a high-risk trade on a 25 times gearing. His ZAR5,000.00 position had a risk exposure of ZAR100,000.00.
- He entered a trade in a share trading at 11 cents. His analysis suggested that the company was about to undertake "some major corporate deal." In fact, the company announced that it was moving from its current sector to the JSE's Main Board. The share jumped to 75 cents.
- That +500% increase turned Jackson's High Risk position as follows:
  - ZAR5,000.00 on 25 times gearing: Exposure of ZAR100,000.00
  - INCOME = 500% on ZAR100,000.00 = ZAR500,000.00.
  - PROFIT = He turned his ZAR5,000.00 into ZAR500,000.00.
  - This is a 10,000% profit.

Note that trading takes discipline, Jackson adheres to his strict entry and exit strategies and thus regularly turns small trades into small profits. The short 2.5 hours trading window reduces his risk exposure.

APPENDICES

The SEC Rules for Penny Shares

In the U.S.A. penny shares can be traded as either over-the-counter securities or on securities exchanges.

It must be noted that trading penny shares must comply with the requirements of Section 15(h) of the SEC Act of 1934, which states that a broker must:

- First approve customers for specific penny share transactions.
- Customers must send the broker a written agreement to the transaction.
- The broker must send the customer a disclosure agreement that sets out potential risks of investing in penny shares.
- This disclosure must set out current market buy-sell signals and market liquidity, if any, for the penny share.
- The broker must set out costs associated to the transaction.
- After the deal has been executed, the broker must send its customers a monthly account statement showing the market value of each penny share held in the customer's portfolio.

For more information about SEC Rules: https://www.sec.gov

Global Stock Exchanges

The following is by no means the only Stock Exchanges available in the selected regions.

AFRICAN STOCK EXCHANGES

Botswana	Botswana Stock Exchange
Ghana	Ghana Stock Exchange
Kenya	Nairobi Stock Exchange
Malawi	Malawi Stock Exchange
Morocco	Casablanca Stock Exchange
Nigeria	Nigerian Stock Exchange
South Africa	The South African Futures Exchange
	The South African Bond Exchange
	JSE Securities Exchange
Zambia	Lusaka Stock Exchange
Zimbabwe	Zimbabwe Stock Exchange

ASIAN STOCK EXCHANGES

Australia	Sydney Futures Exchange
	Australian Stock Exchanges
China	Shenzhen Stock Exchange
Hong Kong	Stock Exchange of Hong Kong
	Hong Kong Futures Exchange
India	National Stock Exchange of India
	Bombay Stock Exchange
Indonesia	Jakarta Stock Exchange
	Indonesia NET Exchange
Japan	Nagoya Stock Exchange
	Osaka Securities Exchange
	Tokyo Grain Exchange
	Tokyo International Financial Futures Exchange
	Tokyo Stock Exchange
Korea	Korea Stock Exchange
Malaysia	Kuala Lumpur Stock Exchange
New Zealand	New Zealand Stock Exchange
Pakistan	Karachi Stock Exchange
	Lahore Stock Exchange
Singapore	Stock Exchange of Singapore
	Singapore International Monetary Exchange Ltd
Sri Lanka	Colombo Stock Exchange
	Sri Lanka Stock Closings
Taiwan	Taiwan Stock Exchange
Thailand	The Stock Exchange of Thailand

EUROPEAN STOCK EXCHANGES

Austria	Vienna Stock Exchange
Belgium	Easdaq
Croatia	Zagreb Stock Exchange
Czech Republic	Prague Stock Exchange
Denmark	Copenhagen Stock Exchange
Finland	Helsinki Stock Exchange
France	Paris Stock Exchange
	LesEchos
	NouveauMarche
	MATIF
Germany	Frankfurt Stock Exchange
Greece	Athens Stock Exchange
Hungary	Budapest Stock Exchange
Italy	Italian Stock Exchange
Lithuania	National Stock Exchange of Lithuania
Macedonia	Macedonian Stock Exchange
The Netherlands	Amsterdam Stock Exchange
Norway	Oslo Stock Exchange
Poland	Warsaw Stock Exchange
Portugal	Lisbon Stock Exchange
Romania	Bucharest Stock Exchange
Russia	Russian Securities Market News
Slovenia	Ljubljana Stock Exchange, Inc.
Spain	Barcelona Stock Exchange
	Madrid Stock Exchange
	Spanish Financial Futures & Options Exchange
Sweden	Stockholm Stock Exchange
Switzerland	Swiss Exchange
Turkey	Istanbul Stock Exchange
United Kingdom	FTSE International (London Stock Exchange)
	London Stock Exchange: Daily Price Summary
	Electronic Share Information
	London Metal Exchange
	London International Financial Futures and Options Exchange

MIDDLE EASTERN STOCK EXCHANGES

Israel	Tel Aviv Stock Exchange
Jordan	Amman Financial Market
Lebanon	Beirut Stock Exchange
Palestine	Palestine Securities Exchange
Turkey	Istanbul Stock Exchange

NORTH AMERICAN STOCK EXCHANGES

Canada	Alberta Stock Exchange
	Montreal Stock Exchange
	Toronto Stock Exchange
	Vancouver Stock Exchange
	Winnipeg Stock Exchange
	Canadian Stock Market Reports
	Canada Stockwatch
Mexico	Mexican Stock Exchange
US	AMEX
	New York Stock Exchange (NYSE)
	NASDAQ
	The Arizona Stock Exchange
	Chicago Board Options Exchange
	Chicago Board of Trade
	Chicago Mercantile Exchange
	Kansas City Board of Trade
	Minneapolis Grain Exchange
	Pacific Stock Exchange
	Philadelphia Stock Exchange

SOUTH AMERICAN STOCK EXCHANGES

Bermuda	Bermuda Stock Exchange
Brazil	Rio de Janeiro Stock Exchange
	Sao Paulo Stock Exchange
Cayman Islands	Cayman Islands Stock Exchange
Chile	Chile Electronic Stock Exchange
	Santiago Stock Exchange

Colombia	Bogota Stock Exchange
	Occidente Stock exchange
Ecuador	Guayaquil Stock Exchange
Jamaica	Jamaica Stock Exchange
Nicaragua	Nicaraguan Stock Exchange
Peru	Lima Stock Exchange
Trinidad and Tobago	Trinidad and Tobago Stock Exchange
Venezuela	Caracas Stock Exchange
	Venezuela Electronic Stock Exchange

Six Ratio Areas

Area	Ratios	Calculation of Ratio
Solvency	General solvency check	[(Fixed assets + investments + current assets) ÷ (long-term loans + current liabilities)] × 100
Liquidity	Current asset ratio	Current assets ÷ current liabilities
	Quick ratio {Acid test)	(Current assets − stock) ÷ current liabilities
	Stock to working capital ratio	(Stocks net current assets) ×100
	Defensive interval ratio	Defensive assets ÷ projected daily operating expenses
Profitability	Profit margins	(Any profit figures turnover) × 100
	Return on shareholders' equity	(Attributable profits ÷ shareholders' funds) × 100
	Return on net assets	(Attributable profits ÷ net assets) × 100
	Return on capital employed	(Operating income ÷ capital employed) × 100
Efficiency	Stock turn • Accounts receivable days • Accounts payable days	Group turnover ÷ average stock Accounts receivable + (turnover +365) Accounts payable + (turnover − 5 − 365)

Area	Ratios	Calculation of Ratio
Leverage	Debt:equity (gearing)	[(Long and short term loans ÷ overdraft − cash) ÷ ordinary shareholders' funds] × 100
	Proportional debt ratio	Long-term ÷ loans total assets
	Ordinary shareholders' interest	(Ordinary shareholders' funds ÷ loans) × 100
	Long-term debt to capital employed	(Long-term loans ÷ capital employed) × 100
	Interest cover	Pretax income ÷ interest paid
	Average interest rate	(Interest expense − accounts payable) ÷ liabilities
	Gross cash flow to total debt ratio	[Gross cash flow (prior dividends) ÷ loan] × 100
	Cash flow to assets	Cash from operations + total assets
	Earnings per share	(Attributable profit ÷ issued orders) × 100
Investment Performance Ratios	Dividend per share	(Dividends payable ÷ issued orders) × 100
	Dividend cover	Earnings per share ÷ dividend per share
	Earnings yield	(Earnings per share ÷ share price) × 100
	Dividend yield	(Dividend per share ÷ share price) × 100
	Dividend payout ratio	Yearly dividend per share ÷ EPS
	Price:earnings ratio	Inverse of earnings yield
	Price earnings growth (PEG)	Price:earnings ÷ company's projected year-over-year earnings growth rate
	Book value per share	(Shareholders' equity − preferred stock) ÷ average outstanding shares
	Debt/asset ratio	Total liabilities ÷ total assets

Glossary

Acceptance date: Time limit given to a prospective shareholder to accept an offer of shares in a rights issue.

Account: A trading period whose dates are fixed by the stock exchange authorities.

Accounts payable: Bills that have to be paid as part of the normal course of business.

Accounts receivable: Debt owed to your company from credit sales.

Acid Test: A ratio used to determine how liquid a company is. It is determined by subtracting short-term assets from accounts receivable and inventory, which is then divided by short-term liabilities.

Aftermarket Performance: A term typically referring to the difference between a stock's Offering Price and its current market price.

Agent: Where a member acts on behalf of a client and has no personal interest in the order.

AIM: The UK-based AltX version, called the Alternative Investment Market.

All or Nothing: means the full order must be executed immediately or, if it is not possible to do so, the order must be routed to the special terms order book.

Allotment Letter: Formal letter sent by a company to the investor to confirm that it will allocate him shares in a new issue.

Alpha: The first version of product where all of the intended functionality has been implemented but interface has not been completed and bugs have not been fixed.

AltX: The new Alternative Exchange launched in South Africa in October 2003.

American depositary receipts (ADRs): Non-U.S. companies who want to list on a U.S. exchange offer these. Rather than constituting an actual share, ADRs represent a certain number of a company's regular shares.

Analyse: The first phase in many developmental and delivery methodologies. The Analyse phase involves examination of the proposal to determine the requirements and "what" is to be addressed by the project.

Annuity: A contract sold to an individual by an insurance company that is designed to provide payments to the holder at specified intervals, generally after retirement.

Arbitrage: A purchase or sale by a member on his/her own account of securities on one stock exchange with the intent to sell or buy those securities on another stock exchange to profit by the difference between the prices of those securities on such stock exchanges.

Arbitrageur: Someone who practices arbitrage.

Asset allocation: The process of dividing investments into different categories, such as stocks, bonds, cash, and real estate.

Asset swap: A transaction which complies with all the requirements of the South African Reserve Bank in respect of an asset swap.

Asset turnover: Sales divided by total assets. Important for comparison over time and to other companies of the same industry.

Assumptions: Statements describing situations that are taken to be true.

At Best: An order to be transacted in a manner that will, in the discretion of the member executing the order, achieve the best price for the client.

At market: An order to be transacted immediately against the best opposite order in the order book at the time of making such entry.

At the Close Order: An order which is to be executed as close to the end of the trading day as possible.

At the Money Option: An option with an exercise price equal to that of the underlying security.

At the Opening Order: An order to buy or sell at a limited price on the initial transaction of the day.

Authorized/issued share capital: While the authorized share capital is the maximum number of shares a company is permitted to issue over time, the issued share capital is the actual number of shares in issue.

Average: A select sampling of stocks used to reflect the basic trends of the market or a specific portion of the market, for example the All Share Index. The average is derived by taking the sum of the market value of the selected stocks and dividing that number by the number of issues or by a divisor that allows for stock splits or other changes in capitalization.

Bad debts: An amount payable by debtors, which the firm determines is irrecoverable.

Balance Order: The pairing off of buy and sell orders of the same security to determine the net balance of securities to receive or deliver. This information allows the market to be opened appropriately.

Balance Sheet: A statement that shows a company's financial position on a particular date.

Bar Chart: A chart used to plot stock movements using vertical bars to indicate prices.

Baseline: A snapshot at a particular point in time of part of a project plan. A "schedule baseline" is a snapshot of the schedule at that point in time. Can be compared over time.

Bear Sales: The sale of listed securities of which the seller is not the owner at the date of sale.

Bear trend: When supply of shares outstrips demand and prices start to fall. If this trend continues for a number of weeks, the general sentiment becomes bearish and prices continue to fall.

Bearish: Used to voice an opinion in the belief that the stock market or some aspect of it is going to decline in price.

Best Efforts: This term is used to describe a deal in which underwriters only agree to "do their best" in selling shares to the public. An IPO is more commonly done on a Bought or Firm Commitment basis in which the Underwriters are obligated to sell the allotted shares.

Beta: The first version of a product where all of the functionality has been implemented and the interface is complete but the product still has problems or defects.

Bid (buyer's price): Offer to buy a number of securities at a certain stated price.

Bid, Not Offered: When shares are sought, but none are available. The opposite would be "offered, not bid."

Big Blue: Nickname for the IBM Corporation. Derived from the color of their logo.

Big Board: Nickname for the New York Stock Exchange.

Big-Bang: The implementation of a new system "all at once" differs from incremental in that the transition from old to new is (effectively) instantaneous.

Black Box Testing: Testing a product without knowledge of its internal working. Performance is then compared to expected results to verify the operation of the product.

Black Monday: A name given to October 19, 1987, when the Dow Jones Industrial Average dropped a record 508 points which represented a decline of almost 23%.

Block: A large amount of securities bought or sold.

Blue Chip Stock: A stock that is from a well-known, stable, prestigious company with a long and successful track record of profit growth and dividend sharing.

Book Value: The net amount of an asset shown in the books of a company, that is, the cost of purchasing a fixed asset less the depreciation on that asset.

Bottom Fishing: Investing in stocks whose prices have dropped dramatically based on the belief that the stock has reached bottom and will now rebound.

Bottom Up: Building or designing a product from elementary building blocks, starting with the smaller elements and evolving into a lager structure.

Brainstorming: A process for generating ideas.

Break-Even Point: The unit sales volumes or actual sales amounts that a company needs to equal its running expenses rate and not lose or make money in a given month. Break-even can either be based on regular running expenses, which is different from the standard accounting formula based on technical fixed expenses.

Breakout: Used to describe when a security rises above or falls below a particular level, generally its previous high or low point.

Broker: The name given to a natural person recognized by the official stock exchange. Institutions have, since 1995, been able to become corporate members.

Brokerage: Commission charged by a member for the purchase or sale of securities.

Broker's Note: a note which a member is required to send to a client recording the details of a purchase or sale of securities.

Bull Market: A market where the dominating trend is one of rising prices.

Bull Trend: When demand for shares outstrips supply and prices start to rise. If this trend continues for a number of weeks, the general sentiment becomes bullish and prices continue to rise.

Bullish: Used to voice an opinion in the belief that the stock market or some aspect of it is going to rise in price.

Buy Stop Order: A buy order that is not to be executed until the market price reaches the customer's defined price, known as the stop price. When this occurs, it becomes a market order.

Buying Power: The amount of additional securities that a customer may purchase using the existing equity in his account.

Call Option: A call option establishes the right to buy a specified quantity of the underlying security at a specified price any time during the duration of the option. You would buy a call option if you expect prices to rise. In South Africa, these are called warrants.

Called Away: Describes a stock option that was sold, because the stock was at or above the strike price.

Capital Assets: Long-term assets, also known as Fixed Assets (plant and equipment).

Capital expenditure: Spending on capital asset (also called plant and equipment, or fixed asset).

Capital input: New money being invested in the business. New capital will increase your cash, as well as the total amount of paid-in capital.

Capital structure: Usually refers to the structure of ordinary and preference shares and long-term liabilities.

Capital Turnover: Annual sales divided by average stockholder equity (net worth) (i.e., total sales for each R1 of equity).

Capital: This is also known as total shares in issue, owner's equity or shareholders' funds.

Capitalization: The total amount of debt and equity issued by a company.

Cash flow: A statement that shows the net difference between cash received and paid during the company's operating cycle.

Cash: The bank balance, or checking account balance, or real cash in bills and coins.

Cash-flow Forecast: An estimate of the timing and amount of a company's inflow and outflow of money measured over a specific period of time; typically, monthly for one to two years, then annually for an additional one to three years.

Churning: When a broker processes excessive trades, regardless of the clients best interest, in an attempt to maximize commissions.

Circuit Breaker: When a halt to trading is implemented for one hour by a major stock or commodity exchange when an index falls a predetermined amount in a session. This is done to prevent further losses.

Close-out Stage: The final project management phase in which the project is evaluated, feedback is elicited, and lessons learned are captured.

Closing Period: The last hour or two of trading before the stock market closes at the end of the day.

Closing price: The last sale price or a higher bid or lower offer price for a particular security.

Collection days: See collection period.

Collection period (days): The average number of days that pass between delivering an invoice and receiving the money.

Commission percentage: An assumed percentage used to calculate commissions expense as the product of this percentage multiplied by gross margin.

Commission: The brokers charge a fee for buying and selling shares, which is brokerage or commission earned on a deal.

Commissions Percent: An assumed percentage used to calculate commissions expense as the product of this percentage multiplied by gross margin.

Commodity futures: A contract to buy or sell a commodity at a specific price and on a specific delivery date.

Common Stock: A securities holding that affords the possessor to have ownership in the company which provides benefits such as voting rights and dividend sharing.

Consumer Price Index: An inflationary indicator that measures the change in the cost of goods and service that the average consumer purchases.

Contingency: Reserve resources (time, effort, or money) that are set aside because of the unpredictability of the future.

Convertible & Redeemable: Preference Shares: An alternative mechanism to ordinary shares. It enables companies to issue other shares, which can either be bought back from investors or converted into ordinary shares at a later date.

Corporate finance transaction: A transaction that is entered into in writing and requires public notification in the press in terms of the listing requirements of an Exchange.

CPI: Abbreviation for Consumer Price Index.

Creditors: People or companies that you owe money to. This is the old name for accounts payable.

Crossed Market: Where a bid price is higher than the offer price for a security.

Cum or ex-dividend: After a company has declared a dividend, it would close its books to start paying dividends. The share will be marked ex-div, which means that any new shareholder will be omitted from the past year's dividend payout. Before the company declares a dividend payout, the share will be assumed to include possible dividends, or to be cum-div.

Current assets: Those assets that can be quickly converted into cash, including accounts receivable, stock and debtors book. These are often called liquid assets.

Current debt: Short-term debt, short-term liabilities.

Current liabilities: A company's short-term debt, which must be paid within the firm's operating cycle, that is, in less than one year.

Day Order: A transaction order that is valid only for the day on which it was entered.

Day Trading: The practice of buying and selling a security on the same day.

Dead Cat Bounce: A quick, moderate rise in the price of a stock following a major decline.

Debentures: A bond that is not secured by fixed assets.

Debt and equity: The sum of liabilities and capital. This should always be equal to total asset.

Debtors: People or companies that owe your company money. It is the old name for accounts receivable.

Deep in the money option: A call option with a strike price that is significantly below the market price or a put option with a strike price that is significantly above the market price.

Delayed Opening: An intentional delay in the start of trading in a stock until a large imbalance in buy and sell orders is eliminated.

Deleted or Delisted: A security that has been removed from public trading.

Delivery date: The date a deliverable is scheduled to be turned over to the next customer in the technical process.

Delta: The change in price of a call option in relation to the change in price of the underlying security.

Depreciation: An accounting and tax concept used to estimate the loss of value of assets over time. For example, cars depreciate with use.

Descending Tops: A chart pattern where each new high price for a security is lower than the previous high.

Dip: A small temporary drop in price during an overall upward trend.

Directive project management: The old management approach in which the project manager did the planning, delegated tasks to team members, monitored the project, and then shut it down.

Discount Rate: A rate of return used to convert a monetary sum, payable or receivable in the future, into present value.

Discounted Cash Flow (DCF): Techniques for establishing the relative worth of a future investment by discounting (at a required rate of return) the expected net cash flow from the project.

Discounting: The process of finding the present value of a series of future cash flows. Discounting is the reverse of compounding.

Divergence in Charting: When two charting lines are heading in opposite directions, generally after a cross-over point.

Diversification: Investing in a wide variety of investments so as to reduce overall risk.

Dividend Coverage: Number of times a company's dividend is covered by earnings available to pay it.

Dividend Yield: Ratio of the latest dividend to the cost or market price of a security expressed as a percentage.

Dividends: Money distributed to the owners of a business as profits.

Double Bottom: When a security has twice declined to its support level.

Double Top: This technical assessment is formed when a stock advances to a certain price level only to retreat from that level, and then rally again back to that level. The up moves are accompanied by high volume and the recession from the top comes on receding volume.

Dow Jones Averages: The most widely used Averages to track overall market conditions. There are four Dow Jones Averages: Industrial, Transportation, Utilities, and Composite. The Composite is simply the previous three combined.

Dow Theory: A theory which is based on the belief that the fluctuations in the stock market are both a reflection of current business trends as well as a predictor of future business trends.

Downtick: A transaction where the stock price is lower than the previous transaction.

Earnings Per Share: Total earnings divided by the number of shares outstanding.

Earnings Yield: Ratio of net earnings per security to the market price expressed as a percentage.

Earnings: Also called income or profits, earnings are the famous "bottom line": sales less costs of sales and expenses.

EBIT: Earnings before interest and taxes.

ECN: Electronic Communication Networks used by day traders and institutions to post bids in the NASDAQ market.

Elliott Wave: A theory of price movement cycles identified by Ralph Elliott. This theory claims that the stock markets follow a pattern of five waves up and three waves down.

EPS: Abbreviation for Earnings per Share.

Equity Buyback: The investors' percentage ownership of a company that can be reacquired by the company, usually at a predetermined amount.

Equity: Business ownership; capital. Equity can be calculated as the difference between assets and liabilities.

Exchange Risk: The risk associated with an asset or liability denominated in a foreign currency. It is vulnerable to the movement of exchange rates.

Ex-Dividend Date: The date at which the Ex-Dividend period begins.

Execution Stage: The stage in the project management process in which the deliverables are created and their progress is tracked.

Executive Summary: A concise summary of an investment proposal that describes a company's background, products or services, financial needs, financial requirements, management capabilities, market description and financial data.

Exercise Date: The date when the sale or purchase of an option occurs as agreed upon in the contract.

Exercise or expiration date: The date when the sale or purchase of an option occurs as agreed upon in the contract.

Exit Options: A variety of options available to investors to recover their invested capital and the return on their investment.

Expected Return: The total amount of money (return) an investor anticipates to receive from an investment.

Expiration Date: The date on which an option becomes worthless if not exercised.

Fair Market Value: A price that both the seller and buyer agree represents a valid price based on current market conditions.

Fill or kill (FOK): The full order must be executed immediately or otherwise canceled.

Final deliverable: The final output from the execution stage of the project that is delivered to the project customer.

Financial notes: Information explaining financial figures (balance sheet, income statement, and cash flow).

Fixed assets: Includes all fixed (immovable) assets, namely property, vehicles, machinery and equipment. It cannot usually be converted into cash within the firm's operating cycle.

Flipping: This is when an investor has acquired an IPO at its offering price and sells it immediately for a quick gain soon after it starts trading on the open market. A practice discouraged by underwriters, it can lead such investors to unfavorable relationships with their underwriters with future IPOs.

Float: The number of shares of a common stock that are outstanding and therefore available for trading by the public.

FOK Order: Abbreviation for Fill or Kill Order.

Forecast: Future-oriented financial information prepared using assumptions, all of which reflect the entity's planned courses of action for the period covered, given management's judgment as to the most probable set of economic conditions.

Foreign Exchange: Claims in a foreign currency payable abroad, including bank deposits, bills, and cheques. Foreign exchange rates refer to the number of units of one currency required to buy another.

Fundamental Analysis: A method of determining a securities value based on the analysis of several factors, such as a company's earnings, sales, assets, and growth potential.

Funding Costs: The price of obtaining capital, either borrowed or equity, with intent to carry on business operations.

Futures: A contract which requires the delivery of a commodity at a specific price on a particular date in the future.

Gantt chart: A schedule that visually shows the duration for each deliverable or activity.

Gap and Trap: The price of stock gaps, buyers purchase the stock. Market makers bring the stock price down, thus trapping the buyers who bought at the higher gap price.

Gap: When the range of a stock price on two successive days does not overlap.

Going concern: A company that is operating, that is, has not stopped producing goods or providing a service, and one which has not been placed under liquidation or curatorship.

Going Public: When a private company first offers shares to the public.

Good till Cancelled Order (GTC): An order which remains valid until executed or canceled by the customer.

Goodwill: An intangible asset reflected in balance sheets, which indicates an excess over market value for assets paid by the firm.

Gross margin percent: Gross margin divided by sales, displayed as a percentage. Acceptable levels depend on the nature of the business.

Gross margin: Sales less cost of sales.

GTC Order: Abbreviation for Good till Canceled Order.

Hammering the Market: Excessive sale of stocks which drives the market down.

Head and shoulders: This technical pattern is typically characterized by one intermediate top, followed by a second top higher than the previous top and a third rally that fails to exceed the head.

Hedge: Taking an investment position in which some investments are designed to offset the risk of others.

Historical data: Data collected from past projects.

Hit the Bid: Immediate sell to the current Bid price.

Hit the Offer: Immediate buy from the current Ask price.

Horizontal Analysis: The process of comparing consecutive financial statements by examining the increases or decreases between the periods in terms of absolute monetary value and percentages.

Hurdle Rate: A predetermined benchmark rate of return. If the rate of return expected from the project or investment falls below the benchmark, the projected investment will no longer be accepted. The hurdle rate should be the marginal cost of capital adjusted for the project's risk.

Hypothecation: The pledge of property and assets to secure a loan. Hypothecation does not transfer title, but it does provide the right to sell the hypothecated property in the event of default.

Immediate deal: A transaction in a listed security where settlement is to take place the next business day.

Implement: The phase of a project involved with delivering the solution to the Business Owner.

In the Money Option: A call option where the strike price is less than the market price or a put option where the strike price is greater than the market price.

Income statement: A statement showing net income or loss for a specified period.

Index Fund: A mutual fund that tries to mirror the performance of a specific index.

Index: A select sampling of stocks used to reflect the basic trends of the market. Indexes are derived from a broader number of stocks than Averages.

Indicator: Statistics which provide an indication of the trends of the financial world or the economy in general.

Initial Public Offering: The first issue and sale of stock by a company to the public.

Insider: A person who is privy to corporate information that is not available to the general public.

Institution: A large organization which is in the business of investing in securities.

Institutional Investors: An entity with a considerable amount of money to invest.

Interest expense: Interest is paid on debts, and interest expense is deducted from profit as expenses.

Internal costs: Expenses for the project that are cross-charged by a department inside the organization.

Intraday: Within a single day.

Intrinsic Value: The amount of money that an option is worth if it was exercised.

Inventory turnover: Sales divided by inventory. Usually calculated using the average inventory over an accounting period, not an ending-inventory value.

Inventory turns: Inventory turnover (see Inventory turnover).

Inventory: This is another name for stock. Goods in stock, either finished goods or materials to be used to manufacture goods.

Investment Banker: An individual or institution which provides services, such as underwriting and counselling, but does not accept deposits or make loans.

IPO: Abbreviation for Initial Public Offering.

Issue: An event that is currently threatening the project and requiring attention.

Issues list: A list to record issues that must be resolved or action items that are not significant enough to put on the project schedule.

Issues Management: A set of practices designed to effectively identify, prioritize, and monitor issues and manage them through to resolution.

Jobbers: These are the market's share merchants. They deal only with brokers and other jobbers (i.e., not with dealers) and their main function is to maintain a market by quoting a price.

Last Sale: The most recent stock trade.

Letter of acceptance: The investor may receive such a letter if the company accepts his or her application for shares.

Leverage Ratio: A financial ratio that measures a firm's debt burden. The debt, times interest earned and fixed charges coverage ratios are leverage ratios.

Leverage: The relationship between interest-bearing debt and equity in a company (financial leverage) or the effect of fixed expense on after-tax earnings (operating leverage).

Leveraged Buyout: Taking over a controlling interest in a company, using primarily borrowed money.

Liabilities: Debts; money that must be paid. Usually debt on terms of less than five years is called short-term liabilities and debt for longer than five years, in long-term liabilities.

Limit order: An order that may only be affected at prices equal to or better than the price on the order.

Limit Price: The price specified in a limit order.

Liquidity: A company's ability to pay short-term debt with short-term assets

Listed Stock: A stock that is traded on a major exchange.

Listing: Official granting of a listing of a company's shares on an Exchange.

Local counterparty transaction: A transaction where a member trades as a principal with a person in South Africa other than a member.

Locked Market: A highly competitive market in which the bids and prices are the same.

Lockup Period: A period of time when a company first goes public during which major shareholders are prevented from selling their shares.

Long Position: When the stock owner is waits for a price move in order to sell at a higher price.

Long-term assets: Assets such as plant and equipment that are depreciated over terms of more than five years, and are also likely to last that long.

Long-term interest rate: The interest rate charged on long-term debt. This is usually higher than the rate on short-term debt.

Long-term liabilities: This is the same as long-term loans. Most companies call a debt long term when it is on terms of five years or more.

MA: Moving Average.

Margin Call: A call from the brokerage to the customer requesting that the customer deposit additional funds into their account in order to return the balance to its required level.

Margin: The amount of money that a customer must deposit with a broker to secure a loan from that broker. In the case of futures, the amount of money that must be deposited to protect the buyer and seller from default.

Market capitalization: Used to denote a company's size, and is calculated by multiplying a company's issued share capital by its current share price.

Market indicators: Statistics that give an overall picture of how the market is performing.

Market Maker Spread: The difference between prices of the market maker closest to the Inside Bid and the market maker closest to the Inside Ask, excluding ECNs.

Market maker: A member who negotiates dealings in blocks of Common stock by always being available to buy or sell at publicly quoted prices.

Market on Close Order: An order to buy or sell that is to be executed during the closing period of the market at the best price available.

Market on the Open Order: An order to buy or sell that is to be executed during the opening period of the market at the best price available.

Market Order: An order to buy or sell stock at the market's current price. Market Value: The latest trading price.

Market Risk: The part of a security's risk that cannot be eliminated by diversification.

Marketable securities tax (MST): The tax imposed in terms of the Marketable Securities Act of 1948 in respect of every purchase of marketable securities through the agency of or from a member at the rate of 0.25% of the consideration for which the securities are purchased.

Marketable Securities: All instruments legally permitted to trade on a country's legitimate stock

Exchange: These include shares (ordinary and preference), gilts, futures, and options.

Materials: Included in the cost of sales. These are not just any materials, but materials involved in the assembly or manufacturing of goods for sale.

Maturity Date: Date on which a debt is due for payment.

Mentor: A close personal contact, usually in your industry, who has a network of contacts in the investment community and can assist in achieving your objectives.

Midday Period: The hours between 11:30 am and 1:30 pm for any trading day. Trade during this time generally slows down as people break for lunch.

Minority Shareholders: Shareholders who by virtue of their percentage ownership of the company do not have voting control of the company.

Minutes: Notes taken during a meeting that summarize discussions and agreed actions.

Momentum Trading: Short to moderate length investments that are made to capitalize on the sudden rise or drop in a stock price that follows certain technical indicators.

Monopoly: When one company controls and dominates a particular market sector or product.

Mortgage: Debt instrument by which the borrower (mortgagor) gives the lender (mortgagee) a lien on property as security for the repayment of a loan

Most Active: Stocks with the day's highest trading volume.

NASD: National Association of Securities Dealers, an organization responsible for regulating the Nasdaq stock market.

NASDAQ: Abbreviation for National Association of Securities Dealers Automated Quotations.

Net Cash Flow: This is the projected change in cash position, an increase or decrease in cash balance.

Net Income: The level of profit in a business after the deduction of income taxes, depreciation, operating expenses, and other expenses. It is also known as after-tax profit or net profit.

Net Present Value (NPV): A method of ranking investment proposals. NPV is equal to the present value of future returns, discounted at the cost of capital, minus the present value of the cost of the investment.

Net profit: The operating income less taxes and interest. The same as earnings, or net income.

Net Realizable Value: Selling price of an asset minus the expenses of bringing the asset into a saleable state and expenses of the sale.

Net worth: This is the same as assets minus liabilities, and the same as total equity.

NYSE Composite Index: An index that measures the market value of all NYSE traded stocks.

NYSE: The New York Stock Exchange where stocks are traded in an open floor market.

Odd Lot: Any quantity of securities which is less than a round lot (Krugerrands do not have odd lots).

Offer (seller's price): Price at which a dealer is prepared to sell securities on the market.

Offering price: This is the price set by the sponsor, at which the company's stock is sold to the first round of investors.

Offering range: This is the price range in which the company expects to sell its stock. This can be found on the front page of the prospectus. As with everything traded, market conditions and demand dictate the final offering price.

Oligopoly: When a few companies control and dominate a particular market.

Open Interest: The number of contracts outstanding at the end of the trading day.

Open Order: An order which remains valid until executed or canceled by the customer.

Opening Price: This is the first price that the company's stock trades on its first day of trading.

Opening price: This is the initial trading price of the company's stock on its first day of trading.

Order: An instruction to buy or sell a specified quantity of a security.

Ordinary Shares: Commercial paper issued to investors to raise capital. Investors hold these shares as part owners in the firm.

OTC: Abbreviation for Over the Counter.

Other short-term assets: These are securities and business equipment.

Other ST liabilities: These are short-term debts that don't cause interest expenses. For example, they might be loans from founders or accrued taxes (taxes owed, already incurred, but not yet paid).

Out of the Money: A call option where the strike price is greater than the market price or a put option where the strike price is less than the market price.

Overheads: Running expenses not directly associated with specific goods or services sold, but with the general running of the business.

Over-the-Counter Market (OTC): A market made up of dealers who make a market for those securities not listed on an exchange.

Paid-in capital: Real money paid into the company as investments. This is not to be confused with par value of stock, or market value of stock. This is actual money paid into the company as equity investments by owners.

Paper profit: A surplus income over expense, which has not yet been released, that is, share prices that have increased above the price at which they were bought, but have not yet been sold.

Paper Trade: Trading stocks for pretend with no real money, to practice or test theories.

Par Value: The nominal value of a share and is an arbitrary amount placed on the share by the company.

Partial Fill: An order that has been implemented for only part of the requested share size.

Payment days: The average number of days that passes between receiving an invoice and paying it.

Payroll burden: Payroll burden includes payroll taxes and benefits. It is calculated using a percentage assumption that is applied to payroll. For example, if payroll is R1 000 and the burden rate 10 percent, and then the burden is an extra R100. Acceptable payroll burden rates vary by market, by industry and by company.

PE Ratio: Abbreviation for price earnings ratio.

Penny Stocks: Low priced, high risk stocks, usually with a price of less than a dollar per share.

Point and Figure Chart: A chart which shows price movements of a security, without measuring the passage of time.

Poison Pill: Any action taken by a company designed to avoid a hostile takeover. For example, issuing preferred stock that can be redeemed at a premium if a takeover does occur.

Portfolio: A schedule, normally computer generated, listing the relevant details in respect of the securities held by an investor.

Preferred Stock: A stock holding which provides a specific dividend that is paid before any dividends are paid to common stock holders. In the event of liquidation, their rights come before common stock holders, but after other holders, such as bond and debt.

Previous Close: The last reported price from the previous trading day. Prints: A price and size report of actual trades in real time.

Price Earnings (P/E) Ratio: The market price of securities divided by its earnings. It expresses the number of years' earnings (at the current rate) which a buyer is prepared to pay for a security.

Primary market: Where shares are distributed at the offering price to investors.

Principal transaction: A member trades with a counterparty or another member.

Principals: The major investors in a corporation. They, generally, have equity interest, voting privileges, access to management records as well as receiving dividends.

Private placement: An offering of a limited amount of shares or units, in which the recipients receive, restricted stock from the issuer.

Product development: Expenses incurred in development of new products; salaries, laboratory equipment, test equipment, prototypes, research and development, etc.

Profit before interest and taxes: This is also called EBIT, for earnings before interest and taxes. It is gross margin minus operating expenses.

Profit Taking: Action by short-term securities traders to cash in on gains created by a sharp market rise. This results in a temporary drop in market prices.

Program Trading: A computerized trading system that allows for large volume securities trading.

Prospectus: This document is an integral part of a documentation that must be filed with the stockbroker. It defines, among many things, the company's type of business, use of proceeds, competitive landscape, financial information, risk factors, strategy for future growth, and lists its directors and executive officers.

Proxy: A person who is authorized to represent another person. For example, a person who is authorized to vote in behalf of another stockholder at a stockholder's meeting.

Rally: A substantial rise in the price level of the overall market, following a decline.

Range: The difference between the highest and lowest prices that are traded during a specific given time frame.

Rate of Return: Return on invested capital (calculated as a percentage). Often an investor has, as one investment criterion, a minimum acceptable rate of return on an acquisition.

Real Time Trade Reporting: When all transactions are instantly requested.

Receivable turnover: Sales on credit for an accounting period divided by the average accounts receivable balance.

Registration: A new shareholder is registered when his or her name is placed on the role of shareholders for that specific company.

Renunciation date: The company sets a date by which the shareholder has to decide whether he or she will take up the rights issue.

Replacement Value: Cost of acquiring a new asset to replace an existing asset with the same functional utility.

Residual Value: Typically estimated based on the present value of the after-tax cash flow expected to be earned after the forecast period.

Resistance: When stocks go up, they tend to reach a point where investors think they are overvalued and sellers of the stock outnumber buyers. This causes the price of the stock to stop dead in its tracks. It cannot go higher because there are no buyers. This point is called "resistance".

Retained earnings: A figure that shows the sum of a company's net profit less dividends paid to shareholders.

Return On Assets: Net profit dividend by total assets. A measure of profitability.

Return on Equity: A ratio used to show how profitable a business is to the shareholders.

Return on investment: Net profits divided by net worth or total equity, yet another measure of profitability. Also called ROI.

Return On Sales: Net profits dividend by sales, another measure of profitability.

Reversal: When the overall market changes directions after a trend in the other direction has occurred.

Reverse Head and Shoulders: This is the same pattern as a head and shoulders except that it has turned upside down and indicates a trend change from down to up. A buy signal is given when prices carry up through the neckline.

Rights Issues: There are a number of methods which a company can use to increase the size of its share capital. If it decides to offer its existing shareholders first option on the issue, it is called a "rights" issue. The dealers would note that such an issue is in progress as it would be quoted as cum-capitalization and after completion of the issue it would be noted as ex-capitalization.

ROI "Return On Investment": A ratio which compares the monetary outlay for a project to the monetary benefit. Used to show success of a project.

Rolling Option: Buying options on a stock that shows a consistent pattern of traveling up and down between two levels.

Round lot: The standard unit of trade in all equities: 100 shares.

Round Trip: The completion of a transaction, which includes both entry into the market and exit.

Rounding Bottom: A chart pattern in the shape of a saucer. Suggesting a new trend upward.

Rounding Top: A chart pattern in the shape of an inverted saucer. Suggesting a new trend downward.

S&P 500: The Standard & Poor index that represents the top 500 value-measured companies.

Scrape Value: An amount left after an asset has been fully depreciated, that is, If an asset of R115 is depreciated by R10 per month over 11 months, the scrape value would be R5

Scrape value: An amount left after an asset has been fully depreciated, that is, if an asset of R115 is depreciated by R10 per month over 11 months, the scrape value would be R5.

SEC: Abbreviation for Securities and Exchange Commission (The USA official stock exchange body).

Secondary market: Better known as the stock market, where shares are openly traded.

Securities: includes stocks, shares, debentures (issued by a company having a share capital), notes, units of stock issued in place of shares, options on stocks or shares or on such debentures, notes or units, and rights thereto, and options on indices of information as issued by a stock exchange on prices of any of the aforementioned instruments.

Sell Stop Order: A sell order which is not to be executed until the market price reaches the customer's defined price, known as the stop price. When this occurs, it becomes a market order.

Selling Off: Selling securities to prevent losses from continued price declines.

Selling on the Good News: Selling a stock right after good news has driven the price very high.

Settlement: Procedure for brokers to close off their books on a particular transaction. The client is expected to pay for his or her new shares on or before the settlement date and he or she, in turn, can expect to be paid (on selling shares) within the same period (also called the settlement period).

Share Capital: Total shares authorized to be issued, or actually issued, by a company.

Shareholders: Owners of one or more shares in a company.

Short Interest: The total number of shares of a security that have been sold short and not yet repurchased.

Short Position: The position that results from short selling that has not yet been covered. Often defined in terms of the number of stocks that are sold short.

Short Sale: Borrowing a security from a broker and selling it, with the understanding that it must later be bought back and returned to the broker.

Short term: Normally used to distinguish between short term and long term when referring to assets or liabilities. Definitions vary because different companies and accountants handle this in different ways. Accounts payable is always short-term assets. Most companies call any debt of less than five-year terms, short-term debt. Assets that depreciate over more than five years (e.g., plant and equipment) are usually long-term assets.

Short-term assets: Cash, securities, bank accounts, accounts receivable, inventory, business equipment, assets that last less than five years or are depreciated over terms of less than five years.

Short-term Gain: A capital gain on an investment which was held for less than six months.

Short-term notes: This is the same as short-term loans. These are debts on terms of five years or less.

Slippage: The difference in price from when an order is placed to when it is actually carried out.

Specialist: A stock exchange member who specialises in particular securities. The specialist must maintain an inventory of those securities and be available to buy and sell shares as necessary to equalize trends and provide an orderly market for those securities.

Splitting of shares: Sometimes a share could become too expensive for the private investor, at which time the company may decide to split or subdivide the shares into smaller denominations. The aim is often to make the shares more tradable and, at times, this increases the share price on positive sentiment.

Sponsor: The person who acts as a liaison between the project leader and the management team, providing oversight to the project.

Spread: The differential between a bid and an offer price.

Stag: An investor who buys shares in a prelisting or rights offer with the intention of selling those shares at a profit as soon as trading starts.

Stakeholder Group: Stakeholders that have similar interests in a project.

Stakeholder: Any person that may have an interest in the process, outputs, or outcomes of a project.

Standard Deviation: A statistical measure of the volatility of a mutual fund or portfolio.

Starting year: A term to denote the year that a company started operations.

Stock Dividend: A dividend paid in shares as opposed to cash.

Stock Exchanges Control Act of 1985 (as amended): An Act of Parliament in terms of which stock exchanges in South Africa are governed. The Financial Services Board administers the Act.

Stocks: A certificate that signifies an ownership position in a company.

Stop Loss Order: A sell stop order for which the specified price is below the current market price. Done to prevent further losses or to lock in profits.

Stop Order: A buy or sell order which is not to be executed until the market price reaches the customer's defined price, known as the stop price. When this occurs, it becomes a market order.

Straddle: The simultaneous purchase of an equal number of puts and calls, with the same strike price and expiration dates.

Strike Price: The specified price at which a call option buyer can buy the underlying security or a put option buyer can sell the underlying security.

Subsidiary: A company in which a majority of the voting shares are owned by another company.

Support: Over time, a stock tends to become attractive to investors at specific prices. When a stock starts to decline to one of these prices, investors tend to come in and purchase the stock, thereby halting its decline. When buyers outnumber sellers, the price of the stock tends to go up. This point at which buyers enter the market is called 'support'.

Surprise: The price difference between what a trader expects to earn and what they actually earn.

Sustainable Growth Rate: The rate of increase in sales a company can attain without changing its profit margin, assets to sales ratios, debt to equity ratio, or dividend payout ratio. It is the rate of growth a company can finance without excessive borrowing or a new stock issue.

Switch Order: An order to sell one security and buy another. Generally, the proceeds from the sale of the first security are used to finance the purchase of the second.

Tax rate percent: An assumed percentage applied against pre-tax income to determine taxes.

Taxes incurred: Taxes owed but not yet paid.

Technical Analysis: Analysing previous market trends and stock prices in the belief that done properly it can be an indicator of future trends.

Tender Offer: A public invitation to stock holders to sell their stock, generally, at a price above the market price. This is done primarily in relation to a takeover.

Tick size: The specified parameter or its multiple by which the price of a security may vary when trading at a different price from the last price, whether the movement is up or down from the last price.

Ticker Symbol: A system of letters used to uniquely identify a stock.

Time of Sales: The actual time and price of transactions as they occur. This information is present on a Level II screen.

Time Value: The difference between an option's intrinsic value and the current market price. The hope being that the intrinsic value over time will go above the market value.

Trading Halt: An interim stop on the trading of a particular stock because of news that might affect either the price of stock, the flow of orders, or even regulatory rule violations.

Trailing Stops: A stop loss order that is to be executed when a stock being followed up, dips down below a specified amount or when a stock being followed down, goes up above a specified amount.

Triple Bottom: A chart pattern that shows that a stock has attempted to penetrate a lower price level on three different occasions.

Two-Sided Market: The NASD and NASDAQ requirement that appropriate bids and offers are made on each security.

Underwriter: An individual or institution which acts as a middle man between corporations issuing securities and the investing public.

Unit variable cost: The specific labor and materials associated with single unit of goods sold. Does not include general overhead.

Units break-even: The unit sales volume at which the fixed and variable costs are exactly equal to sales.

Uptick: A transaction where the stock price is higher than the previous transaction.

Volume: The number of shares traded during a defined period.

What If Scenarios: Analysis of the economic effect of possible future situations, such as economic downturns, loss of key customers, changes in interest rates or price levels, or new competitors or technologies.

White Knight: An investor who prevents a hostile takeover, by taking over the target company himself.

Suggested Readings

Anuff, Joey and Gary Wolf: *Dumb Monday: Adventures of a Day Trader*. New York: Random House, 2000.

Armen, A and Allan, WR: *University Economics, 3rd ed.,* Wadsworth Publishing Company, 1972. Belmont, United States

Associated Press: *World Currencies Roiled by China Currency Talk*. People's Daily Newspaper, May 11, 2005.

Basso, Thomas: *Panic-Proof Investing*: John Wiley & Sons Inc, 1994. New York, United States

Bentley, Kassandra. *Getting Started in Online Day Trading*. John Wiley & Sons, 2000. New York, United States

Bergen, K: *New Opportunities, but Dangers Still Lurk for Many Investors*. Chicago Tribune, 1999.

Bierovic, Thomas: *Playing for Keeps in Stocks & Futures: Three Top Trading Strategies That Consistently Beat the Markets*. John Wiley & Sons, 2001. New York, United States

Bloom, Howard: The Lucifer Principle. Atlantic Monthly Press, 1995. New York, United States

Bookstaber, Richard: *Option Pricing and Investment Strategies, 3rd ed*, Chicago: Pro-bus Publishing, 1991.

Brett, M: *How to Read the Financial Pages*. Random House Business Books, 2003. Westminster, United States

Briese, Stephen E: *The Inside Track to Winning*. Financial trading, 1993. New York, United States

Brigham, E: *Essentials of Management Finance, 3rd ed.* Dryden Press, 1983. Chicago, United States

Browne, Andrew: *How a News Story, Translated Badly, Caused Trading Panic*. The Wall Street Journal, May 12, 2005, p. A1. The Wall Street Journal, 1211. New York, United States

Buckman, R: *These Days, Online Trading Can Become An Addiction*. The Wall Street Journal, 1999. New York, United States

Carrie, L:*Interactive Edition*, The Wall Street Journal, 1998 to 2007. New York, United States

Cambridge University Economic Department: *Ricardo, D - Principles of Political Economy and Taxation*. Cambridge University Press, 1962. Cape Town, South Africa.

Carter, John: *Mastering the Trade*. McGraw-Hill, 2005. New York, United States

Chande, Tushar S., and Stanley Kroll: *The New Technical Trader*. John Wiley & Sons, 1994. New York, United States

Costello, M: *Day-Trading Gurus Tell All*. CNNFN - The Financial Network, 1998.

Emshwiller, J: *Inside the Wild & Wooly World of Internet Stock Trading*. HarperBusiness, 2000. New York, United States

Farrell, Christopher A: *Day Trade Online*. John Wiley & Sons Inc., 2001. New York, United States

Douglas, Mark: *The Disciplined Trader*. Institute of Finance, 1990. New York, United States

Douglas, Mark: *Trading in the Zone*. NJ: Prentice-Hall: Englewood Cliffs, 2001.

Hamilton, W: *The Day-Trading Craze: Whose Crisis is This?* Los Angeles Times, 1999.

Helmkamp, John: *Principles of Accounting,* John Wiley & Sons, 1982. New York, United States

Hyuga, Takahiko: *UBS to Return Money from Tokyo Trading Error*. Bloomberg News, International Herald Tribune, Thursday, December 15, 2005.

IMF Research Department: *World Economic Outlook*, IMF, 2010.

Jurik, M: *Computerized Trading: Maximizing Day Trading and Overnight Profits*. USA: Penguin, 1999

Kahn, Michael: *Technical Analysis Plain and Simple: Charting the Markets in Your Language. 2nd Edition*, Financial Times Prentice Hall, 2006.

Magliolo, J: *Become Your Own Stockbroker*. Zebra Press, 2005. South Africa.

Magliolo, J: *Share Analysis And Company Forecasting*. Struik Zebra Press, 1995. South Africa.

Magliolo, J: *The Millionaire Portfolio*. Struik Zebra Press, 2002. South Africa.

Millman, Gregory J: *The Day Traders: The Untold Story of the Extreme Investors and How They Changed Wall Street Forever*. New York: Times Business, 1999.

Moffett, Sebastian: *Japanese Economic Growth May Not Translate to Stocks*. The Wall Street Journal, January 6, 2006, p. C14. New York, United States

MoneyWeek: *What Was Your Worst Day at Work? Not as Bad as This..."* December 9, 2005.

Orley, MA, Jr: *A Pedestrian's Guide to Economics*. Oklahoma State University Press, 1994. Oklahoma, United States

Owen F: *Understanding Exchange Rates*. Federal Reserve Bank of Cleveland, 1998.

Peters E: *Chaos and Order in the Capital Markets*. John Wiley & Sons, 1992. New York, United States

Peters E: *Fractal Market Analysis*. John Wiley & Sons, 1994. New York, United States

Richardson, P: *Globalisation and Linkages: Macro-Structural Challenges and Opportunities.* OECD Economic Studies, 1997.

Robinson, G: *Strategic Management Techniques.* Butterworths, 1986. Canada

Samuelson, Paul: *Is Real-World Price a Tale Told by the Idiot of Chance?* Review of Economics and Statistics, 58(1), 1976, pp. 120–123.

Schwager, Jack: *Market Wizards: Interviews with Top Traders.* HarperCollins Publishers, 1990. New York, United States

Sexton, D & Kasarda, J: *The State of the Art of Entrepreneurship*, KWS-Kent, 1992.

Silver, David: *A Venture Capital: The Complete Guide for Investors.* John Wiley & Sons, 1985. New York, United States

Weiss, J: *A Framework for Strategic Planning to Support Strategic Management.* Chase Manhattan Bank, 1980.

Other works by the Author

- *Share Analysis & Company Forecasting* (Struik Business Library, 1995)
- *The Business Plan: A Manual for South African Entrepreneurs* (Zebra Press, 1996)
- *The Millionaire Portfolio* (Zebra Press, 2003)
- *Jungle Tactics: Global Research, Investment & Portfolio Strategies* (Heinemann, 2003)
- *A Guide to AltX: Listing on SA's Alternative Stock Exchange* (Zebra, 2004)
- *Become Your Own Stockbroker* (Zebra, 2005)
- *The Corporate Mechanic: The Analytical Strategist's Guide* (Juta, 2007)
- *Richer Than Buffett: Day Trading to Ultra-Wealth* (Struik, 2007)
- *The Guerrilla Principle: Winning Tactics for Global Project Managers* (Juta, 2008)
- *Women & Wealth* (Oshun, 2009)
- *Lore of the Global Trader* (Penguin, 2011)
- *Master Trader* (Penguin, 2011)
- *Business & Entrepreneurship* (Milpark Business School, 2013)

Index

OTHER TITLES IN OUR FINANCE AND FINANCIAL MANAGEMENT COLLECTION

John A. Doukas, Old Dominion University, *Editor*

- *Rays of Research on Real Estate Development* by Jaime Luque
- *Introduction to Foreign Exchange Rates, Second Edition* by Thomas J. O'Brien
- *Weathering the Storm: The Financial Crisis and the EU Response, Volume I: Background and Origins of the Crisis* by Javier Villar Burke
- *Weathering the Storm: The Financial Crisis and the EU Response, Volume II: The Response to the Crisis* by Javier Villar Burke
- *Essentials of Retirement Planning: A Holistic Review of Personal Retirement Planning Issues and Employer-Sponsored Plans, Third Edition* by Eric J. Robbins
- *Financial Services Sales Handbook: A Professionals Guide to Becoming a Top Producer* by Clifton T. Warren
- *Money Laundering and Terrorist Financing Activities: A Primer on Avoidance Management for Money Managers* by Milan Frankl and Ayse Ebru Kurcer
- *Designing Learning and Development for Return on Investment* by Carrie Foster

Announcing the Business Expert Press Digital Library

Concise e-books business students need for classroom and research

This book can also be purchased in an e-book collection by your library as

- *a one-time purchase,*
- *that is owned forever,*
- *allows for simultaneous readers,*
- *has no restrictions on printing, and*
- *can be downloaded as PDFs from within the library community.*

Our digital library collections are a great solution to beat the rising cost of textbooks. E-books can be loaded into their course management systems or onto student's e-book readers.

The **Business Expert Press** digital libraries are very affordable, with no obligation to buy in future years. For more information, please visit **www.businessexpertpress.com/librarians**. To set up a trial in the United States, please contact **sales@businessexpertpress.com**.

www.ingramcontent.com/pod-product-compliance
Lightning Source LLC
Chambersburg PA
CBHW062042200326
41519CB00017B/5111